Mexico

An Illustrated History

Mexico

An Illustrated History

MICHAEL BURKE

HIPPOCRENE BOOKS INC.
NEW YORK

ISBN 0-7818-0690-9

For information, address:
HIPPOCRENE BOOKS, INC.
171 Madison Avenue
New York, NY 10016

Library of Congress Cataloging-in-Publication Data
Burke, Michael E., 1942-
  Mexico : an illustrated history / Michael Burke.
        p.   cm.
  Includes index.
   ISBN 0-7818-0690-9
  1. Mexico—History. I. Title
  F1226.B916   1999
  972—dc21   99-25595
                                              CIP

Printed in the United States of America

CONTENTS

INTRODUCTION

Mexico is a land of rich diversity and extraordinary contradictions. Its two thousand-mile border with the United States is the only place on earth where the Third World so directly confronts the First World. In major metropolitan areas one can shop in modern enclosed malls, travel modern expressways, and catch the latest films on cable television. Never far away are Indians just arrived from the countryside wearing their native garb, worshipers attending Mass in seventeenth-century churches, or peasants hauling firewood on burros. Outside the metropolitan areas, the contrasts are even greater. Isolated villages with huts made of adobe or thatch dot the countryside. In the South, many peasants speak native tongues, not Spanish. Yet, along the Pacific and Caribbean coasts are modern luxury resorts, some explicitly designed to attract American tourists, and some among the most modern and luxurious in the world.

Mexico assaults the senses. It would seem Mexicans abhor silence. At all hours of the day and night one hears the cries of vendors selling everything from flowers to Chiclets, trying to attract passers-by, hoping to make enough pesos to make it through another day. Everywhere is the sound of radios and cassette players at full volume, whether it be the sorrowful ranchero music or the latest North American rock. The past and the present similarly contribute to a unique Third World Mediterranean aroma: a combination of olive oil, used everywhere for cooking, and the sweet smell of diesel from trucks and buses.

Despite its huge population, Mexico is still a land of relaxation and escape. Its unspoiled coasts offer not only ultra-modern resorts, but miles of deserted beaches. Rugged mountain ranges divide the country and offer spectacular vistas. In every part of Mexico one can travel for miles without seeing any evidence of human habitation.

Within Latin America, Mexico is a major political and economic power. With a population approaching 90 million, it is the largest Spanish-speaking country in the world. Its capital, Mexico City, with a population exceeding 20 million, is the world's largest metropolis. Yet, when Mexicans direct their thinking outward, they think of the United States, the driving force in its recent history and its present-day reality. Mexicans, through first-hand experience, tourism, and the mass media, know far more about the United States than North Americans know about Mexico. The United States' political agenda defines the issues that divide the two nations, be it oil in the seventies or drugs and immigration today. And within the United States, 20 million Americans trace their ancestry back to Mexico, 8 million of whom were born in Mexico.

It often seems that Mexicans have a love-hate relationship with the United States. They envy our prosperity and productivity; many admire our political system. At the same time, Mexicans find North Americans loud, superficial, materialistic, and too much in a hurry to appreciate such things of the soul as beauty, friends, and mystery. Mexicans are also quick to tell North American friends that while they admire the United States, they disapprove of its government's policy toward Mexico and Latin America. Indeed, as a gesture of its own autonomy, Mexican foreign policy has often gone out of its way to establish an independent path.

The United States government categorizes Mexico as an "advanced developing country." Mexico has a huge industrial base, making it all but self-sufficient in consumer goods. Over two-thirds of its people live in urban areas. It boasts a substantial middle class, which patronizes modern shopping centers, drives new automobiles, and sends its children to universities. Yet, Mexico is also a poor country. Over 40 percent of its adult population is unemployed or underemployed. The legal minimum wage, not always enforced, is less per day than is the United States minimum wage per hour. Per capita income is less than $2,000 per year; even this figure is deceptively optimistic, since income distribution is among the most inequitable in the Western Hemisphere.

Mexico's poor, however, do not to lack dignity; for, Mexicans have never associated self-worth with material possessions. In addition, Mexico is a country of uncommon ingenuity, an ingenuity born of desperation. (If there is laziness, one of many unfortunate and erroneous stereotypes held by North Americans, it exists among the wealthy, not the poor.) In every city, most especially in Mexico City, one finds men and women of all ages, some as young as four and five, in the streets trying to make a living at all hours of the day and night. Many are street vendors, selling everything from tourist memorabilia to common household goods. Others entertain passers-by, hoping for a few pesos. Older women with young children can only beg.

History is everywhere in Mexico, alive and unsanitized. The remains of two thousand year-old indigenous cities rise out of the jungles and mountains. Colonial churches, government buildings, and mansions dominate the downtowns of most cities. Mexico's past is not preserved as relics, however; Indian ruins become weekend playgrounds, and colonial structures are still in use as administrative centers, places of worship, corporate headquarters, and hotels. Mexico has not just preserved its past; it inhabits it.

9

Modern Mexico was born of conquest. Spanish conquistadors overthrew mighty indigenous civilizations. The culture that resulted, however, was neither Spanish nor Indian; Mexico today is a fusion of the two, a *mestizo* nation, with proud roots in both the indigenous and the Spanish. Racial designations—Indian, white—have become cultural terms. Mexican Catholics attend Mass on the same sites where their ancestors once worshiped indigenous gods on mighty pyramids.

Thoughtful Mexicans have long been preoccupied with their identity. What does it mean to be Mexican? Who are the heros from the past? Is the modern Mexican a relic of past cultures, or a symbol for the future, where diverse peoples and cultures fuse together in one universal race? In a world that too often emphasizes differences, Mexico can teach us the value of a common identity in which no culture is excluded.

If Mexico's cultural identity is one of fusion, its political identity is one of contradictions. Mexico's historical heroes are revolutionaries who were dedicated to radically altering the social and economic structure of their country. The history of Mexico is one of an enduring social order, marked far more by violence than by change. The twentieth century opened with social revolution. Politicians still trace their roots back to the Revolution. Contemporary Mexico, however, remains a one-party state, where government, business, and labor leaders collaborate in maintaining their special privileges. A rich historical legacy takes on a life of its own, all but immune from reality.

In Mexico history matters! It is not only the story of how the present came to be, but the explanation of present realities and future possibilities. Historical issues are debated in the popular press; historical interpretations define contemporary ideological positions. History places limits on the future.

The history of the United States is usually told as a success story. Once the nation identified problems, it proceeded to solve them. Countless memorials and monuments celebrate the success of many battles fought and won by the United States.

In contrast, Mexican history is a series of tragedies, with few happy endings. It is the story of successive conquests, and economic dependency. The Aztecs destroyed local autonomy. Spain destroyed a civilization. The United States took half of Mexico's territory, and France imposed a monarchy. First England, then the United States, dominated economic life. Noble efforts at reform fell short, often as not because of personal ambitions and greed. It is not surprising, then, that, for Mexicans, history must be transcended, not fulfilled.

The history of Mexico is the story of domination, not only foreign, but of individuals and cities within Mexico. Much of that country's history is the story of larger-than-life individuals who, through a combination of sheer will power and political acumen, time and again changed the direction of Mexico: Hernán Cortés who with five hundred men conquered an empire of millions; Miguel Hidalgo who started the drive for independence; Santa Ana, who dominated a half century of Mexican political life and lost half his country to the United States; the revolutionary folk-heroes Poncho Villa and Emiliano Zapata. In Mexico individuals have always been more important than institutions or laws. Mexican history is also the story of Mexico City (Tenochtitlán under the Aztecs), the longest continually-occupied capital in the Western hemisphere which, for more than seven centuries, has dominated the political, economic, and cultural life of the nation.

PRE-COLUMBIAN MEXICO

The Mexicans of today can trace their roots back thousands of years. While Greek and Roman civilization were flourishing in the Mediterranean, Mexicans were building large cities and constructing vast temples and pyramids in Mesoamerica.

The history of Mexico before the arrival of the Europeans is a complex one. Civilizations did not suddenly spring up, only to disappear a few centuries later; rather, the story of pre-Columbian Mexico is one of continuity, as a variety of similar civilizations rose to prominence at different times in distinct areas of Mexico. Migrations, usually from the north, brought new ideas, even as these new arrivals were themselves influenced by the cultures they encountered. In other words, the indigenous culture of Mexico reflected the fusion of many different influences over hundreds of years. Since many of the sacred pre-Columbian cities whose remains visitors explore today retained their special status over many years, they are frequently an amalgamation of different cultures and different influences.

INDIGENOUS SOCIETY

When the Spaniards entered the Aztec capital in 1519 they were amazed at its size and beauty. Little did they realize that they were witnessing the culmination of centuries of Native American civilization.

In present-day Mexico, archaeologists have found traces of human habitation that date as far back as 50,000 B.C. Agriculture and village society had evolved by 1500 B.C. Ancient Mexican society reached its height between 200 B.C. and A.D. 900 in the so-called Classic Period. (Earlier writers referred to this period as the Theocratic Period.) It was during this time that grand cities and religious centers were constructed in Central Mexico, the Yucatán, and in Guatemala. The civilizations of the Classic Period were also renowned for their advances in science and the arts. Toward the end of the Classic Period, new waves of migrations from the north overwhelmed the declining Classic states. These post-Classic societies were more warlike and more committed to human sacrifice. At the same time, they absorbed much of the Classic culture that had preceded them.

Throughout pre-Columbian history, Mexico was predominantly a society of peasants, who lived off the land. Mexican peasant society was based on communities, not individuals. These individuals identified themselves not in terms of their own achievements or possessions, but as members of a particular family or village. Families lived together in villages, not apart from each other on their own plots of land. Indeed, land was owned by the village, not by individuals, even though individual households might be assigned specific plots of land to use. In other words, private property as it is known today—that is, property owned by a person to use or sell as desired—did not exist. Access to property, as distinct from ownership, was determined by need and usage, and was always contingent upon the greater needs of the community.

The religious beliefs of Mexico's Native American cultures were complex, comprehensive, and coherent. It is a serious mistake to view pre-Columbian theology as a simplistic collection of isolated myths and repulsive ceremonies. Rather, indigenous theology dealt with the same ultimate questions every human being must confront: the nature of good and evil, the origins of creation and of human beings, the nature of life and death, and the human being's hope, individually and collectively, to influence those forces beyond his/her control. To view indigenous religious beliefs as nothing more than curious mythology is analogous to reducing Christianity to a few parables of Jesus, or stories of saints. Indeed, Native Americans became as adept at synthesizing sovereignty and religion, ideals and self-interests, as European Christians.

The world was a fearsome place for pre-Columbian Mexico, filled with sinister forces that somehow must be controlled. Evil lurked potentially in every insect and animal. Human beings had little control over their destinies, but were at the mercy of forces more powerful than themselves. Only by appeasing the most potent of these forces could human beings find any security.

Like most agricultural societies, the peoples of Mexico were both fascinated and terrified by the cycles of day and night and of the seasons. In Mexico, where it generally rains only between May and August, there was the additional cycle of rainy season and dry season. To this set of natural cycles was added the metaphysical cycle wherein creation itself consisted of a series of cycles, at the end of which life might or might not be renewed. The Aztec version, which consisted of fifty-two year cycles, was particularly frightening since few would avoid the real possibility of the end of all existence at least once in their lifetimes.

The purpose of religion, then, was renewal and re-creation. It was not inevitable that the rainy season would arrive once again, or that life itself would continue. These required the active participation of the supernatural. Only by serving the deities that governed the cycles and by rendering sacrifices to them would continuity be assured. Without the gods, human activity was useless.

Thus, it is not surprising that the great civilizations of the Classic era were dominated by priests, and their cities dominated by temples. What could provide greater legitimacy to a ruling class than the ability to comprehend the wishes of the gods and thereby preserve all existence? In every pre-Columbian culture, religion provided the basis of sovereignty and justified the status quo.

Human sacrifice was a crucial component of pre-Columbian religion, a practice that had its own logic. What greater sacrifice can human beings make to their gods than to sacrifice their own? Anything less would be less than total subservience. Human sacrifice is less reflective of a barbarism than of a world in which the supernatural is all-powerful and human beings have virtually no power at all. Although the evidence is sparse, it seems probable that in many cases individuals voluntarily offered themselves as victims, or at least took pleasure in the chance to make the ultimate sacrifice for the larger community. Human sacrifice was not simple killing; it occurred at special times in special places, and was surrounded with much ritual.

Indigenous theology allowed for an infinite number of deities, some more powerful than others, some more favored than others. To worship one was not to deny the existence of others, but only to recognize his special powers—and the power of those who promoted his cult. Certain deities, however, dominated the Mexican pantheon everywhere.

Tlaloc, the god of rain, was worshiped throughout Mexico, since it was he who assured the return of the rainy season. Only human victims would guarantee his cooperation. Among the Maya, victims were hurled into the sacred cenotes, in effect to the water itself.

The most fascinating deity, whose cult has deep roots in both the Monte Albán and Teotihuacan cultures was Quetzalcoatl. Whereas most gods were of nature, Quetzalcoatl represented civilization. It

Tlaloc, the rain god for the peoples of central Mexico.

Façade of the Temple to Quetzalcoatl, Teotihuacan. (This façade was once covered by an additional pyramid.)

was Quetzalcoatl who fostered agriculture, industry, and learning. Indeed, Quetzalcoatl represented a kind of hope, an escape from the dominance of a sinister nature. Quetzalcoatl alone rejected human sacrifice, preferring such symbolic sacrifices as butterflies or birds.

The religion of indigenous Mexico left not only spectacular ruins, but also a set of attitudes that explain much of that country's more recent history. Its fatalism, its resignation to adversity, are not conducive to revolution. A people whose deepest instincts associate change with disaster and look upon stability as the best one can hope for will have modest hopes for a better world.

From time to time over many centuries, large city-states arose. Some were commercial centers, others religious centers. Most developed a privileged class of priests, governors, and merchants. The city-states attempted to exert influence over the surrounding countryside, and forced villages to pay tribute and to provide labor for public buildings and temples. Peasants were obligated to worship the gods of the city-state in addition to their own. Religion, then, became the dynamism that compelled obedience. In other words, the wealth and achievements of the cities were possible only through the exploitation of the surrounding villages. This legacy helps to explain the preferred isolation of many remote villages, and their reluctance to welcome the representatives of outside authority, no matter how well-intentioned they might be.

As we look at the principal pre-Columbian civilizations of Mexico, it is important to keep in mind two things: first, the majority of Mexicans continued to live simple lives in small rural villages; and second, as one center of culture followed another in preeminence, the inhabitants of the former culture remained, becoming ultimately the Mexicans of today.

The Olmecs

The earliest known civilization was that of the Olmecs, who constructed large ceremonial centers on the Gulf coast in the present states of Vera Cruz and Tabasco. Remains suggest that the jaguar and other feline forms played an important role in theology, perhaps as fertility symbols. Relics from ancient cities also include huge stone heads as high as eight feet, apparently depicting soldiers wearing helmets.

The Olmecs most likely represent the birth of a society divided according to class, wherein a class of priests dominated, monopolized sacred knowledge, and organized the labor of those below. Such an exclusive class of priest-rulers became characteristic of all indigenous cultures that followed, and, arguably, remained characteristic of Mexico well into the nineteenth century.

The Classic Civilizations (200 B.C.–A.D. 900)

Historians have traditionally pointed to the Maya as the preeminent Mexican civilization prior to the arrival of the Aztecs. Modern scholarship has revealed that the Maya of the Yucatán and present-day Guatemala were but one segment of a larger Classic civilization that dominated central and southern Mexico between 200 B.C. and A.D. 900. Classic Mexico, for example, possessed a common pantheon of deities, although their names varied from place to place.

The major achievement of Classic society was its great cities. These cities were not only ceremonial centers, as scholars once believed, but also dynamic centers of urban life. Pyramids, rising toward the

Olmec head.

sky and visible from miles away, were constructed so that religious rituals could be held on their flat summits. Important priests, merchants, and other officials lived in palaces near the temples. The working class most likely lived in small huts on the outskirts of the city. Urban life was enhanced with broad boulevards and sophisticated water and sewer systems.

Cities of the Classic world dominated the religious and economic life of the surrounding countryside. There is little evidence, however, to suggest that they had to use force to impose their wills; apparently religious belief, combined with the magnetism of these grand centers, generated loyalty.

The cities flourished and expanded over many centuries. Growth was apparently planned according to some grand scheme; unlike modern cities, growth did not just happen. Classic cities exhibit a remarkable sense of space and proportion, a consistency of design, and a grid pattern of strict right angles in the layout of streets and buildings. Their designers maintained a sense of spaciousness despite the immense size of some of the pyramids.

The Classic world is also noteworthy for its scientific and artistic achievements. It possessed a religious elite who preserved thorough historical records, often on stone monuments. The movement of time had a singular fascination for this Classic culture, and was the cause of its principal scientific achievements. Calendars were more precise than those in Europe, marking a year at precisely 365¼ days. Astronomical observatories measured movements of the heavens. The Maya, using a number system based on twenty, developed the concept of zero, a concept Europe did not borrow from the Arabs until well into the Middle Ages.

Both religion and necessity apparently dictated this preoccupation with time. Again, history was divided into a series of fifty-two year cycles. At the end of each cycle, creation was thought to continue only if a deity actively intervened. On a more worldly level, the large regimented society that supported Classic culture required careful planning and management: planting and harvesting must begin on schedule if the society were to feed itself.

The civilization of Classic Mexico developed a complex form of writing; once again, the Maya carried this art the furthest. Numbers were expressed with bars and dots, a bar representing five and a dot one. Glyphs, or symbols, designated both words and phonetic sounds that could be combined to say many different things.

Ritual ball games were an important part of Classic life. In a large submerged court the size of a soccer field, players tried to hit a small, hard ball through a ring high above the playing field. Apparently the outcome of some games was so significant that the captain of the losing team was destined for human sacrifice afterwards.

Despite sophistication in some areas, people of the Classic Period were remarkably lacking in other areas. They never developed the wheel (though archaeologists have uncovered toys with wheels), and they made little use of metals other than for jewelry. Indeed, the lack of both wheeled vehicles and domesticated animals makes the achievements of these cities even more incredible.

The principal sites that fascinate both archaeologists and visitors today were once the religious and political urban centers of this remarkable and mysterious culture. Foremost among these sites, both as powerful cities more than a thousand years ago and as the richest sources of our understanding of those cities today, are, in chronological order: Monte Albán, Teotihuacan, and the Maya ruins in the Yucatán peninsula. All were deserted long before the arrival of the Spaniards, although the descendants of the thousands of peasants who supported their growth and construction still lived in surrounding small villages.

Monte Albán and Teotihuacan

The earliest center of Classic culture was Monte Albán, near the modern city of Oaxaca, some 350 miles south of present-day Mexico City. Here, atop a large hill overlooking the fertile valley below, was constructed a large ceremonial center. The Zapotec people who constructed Monte Albán were the first to develop an accurate 365-day calendar and a primitive form of writing. The construction of the city must have been a formidable task since huge stones had to be transported to the top of the mountain. Construction began as early as the seventh century B.C.

The second major center was that of Teotihuacan, located some twenty miles north of Mexico City. Teotihuacan was the largest of the Classic cities, a vast metropolis consisting of not only countless pyramids and temples, but also luxurious dwellings, marketplaces, and government centers. At the height of its influence, around A.D. 500, its population may have approached 250,000, which would have made it one of the world's largest cities in its day.

Monte Albán and Teotihuacan dominated southern and central Mexico, respectively, from approximately 200 B.C. Both cities grew spectacularly over time, and even the pyramids were expanded by erecting new structures over existing ones. Ancillary cities, such as Mitla near Monte Albán and Cholula near Teotihuacan, arose as the influence of these cities expanded; thus, each of the two cultures, though dominated by a center of political and religious power, encompassed many substantial subordinate cities as well. Toward the end of the Classic Period, both cities were mysteriously deserted—Teotihuacan in A.D. 650, and Monte Albán around A.D. 900. Although it is not known precisely what led to their abandonment, most scholars assume that it was some combination of invasion from the north and a decline in the willingness of peasants from the surrounding area to support the urban centers. In time, many ancillary cities were abandoned as well.

The Maya

Until a generation ago, the Maya world, the best known culture of the Classic world, was seen as a utopia. Unlike their more militaristic neighbors to the north, it was thought that the Maya lived in peace, studying mathematics and contemplating the heavens. Their civilization represented the high point of indigenous culture, a world of autonomous city-states that flourished for centuries, then mysteriously disappeared.

Contemporary scholarship has deprived the Maya of their uniqueness, suggesting that they were but part of the larger Classic culture that dominated Middle America for more than a millennium. What distinguished the Maya culture from that of Teotihuacan and Monte Albán was its lack of a single religious or cultural center. If there was a center to Maya culture, it was probably in the northern Guatemalan province of Petén (although autonomous city-states arose throughout southern Mexico and northern Central America). Indeed, it now appears that this lack of a dominant center made the Maya more warlike than their northern neighbors, as each urban center competed for supremacy. Ruins, for example, illustrate bound prisoners, even human sacrifice.

That the Maya were not exempt from such human qualities as violence and greed should not detract from their achievements. At one time, there were as many as twenty Maya cities, each with more than fifty thousand inhabitants. These were stable, if unequal societies, in which regimentation based on religious belief assured stability and prosperity. ✍

(Modern research has not challenged Maya supremacy in mathematics and astronomy. Their precise calendar fixed the beginning of the world in 3133 B.C.; their system of numbers, based on twenty, allowed for distinct figures to represent huge quantities, one the equivalent of 64 million.) Curiously, their calendar and number system were devised to represent large rather than small amounts. While their calendar could accurately reflect thousands of years, the Maya had little interest in small units of time such as minutes or hours.

The principal archaeological site in Mexico that reflects the Classic period of Maya culture is Palenque, a city of temples and decorative pyramids surrounded by jungle. Uxmal, more modest in scope, is easily accessible from Mérida. Dzibilchaltún is a lesser known but more important site, located just north of Mérida. Settled as early as 1000 B.C., and still inhabited when the Spanish arrived, Dzibilchaltún is the longest continuously-inhabited city in the Western Hemisphere according to some authorities. Chichén Itzá, on the other hand, the most famous Maya site, was constructed centuries after the Maya civilization had reached its height, although the area was undoubtedly inhabited much earlier.

The Post-Classic Period

By the year A.D. 900, Classic culture everywhere was in decline. The great cities of Monte Albán and Teotihuacan were deserted relics of an earlier time, as were many of the grand cities of the

Maya. One can only speculate about the reasons for decline: over-population, climatic changes, social revolt from below against a small, wealthy priestly class. Whatever the causes, the decline opened the way for immigration from the north by less civilized, more militaristic tribes who, in turn, imposed their will on the weakened descendants of the Classic Period.

The next few centuries were a time of synthesis. New arrivals built their own cities, often on the sites of existing ones, sometimes literally so—statuary, temples, and pyramids were erected as outer shells around existing structures. They brought a new social order, dominated by a military elite who used religion to serve their own interests. Human sacrifice, rare during the Classic Period, became common as a means of mass terrorism. In many respects, post-Classic culture resembles the less attractive characteristics of feudal Europe during the same period. Most significantly, the warrior-conquerors of the Post-Classic Period established the form of conquest—imposition of new gods, personal tribute, new cities on top of old—that the Spaniards later emulated with great success.

The Post-Classic Period also marks the beginning of a written historical record, including detailed accounts of individual rulers, families, and conflicts, that enables us to follow specific dynasties and conquests. Even though this record is interwoven with the actions of gods, like similar chronicles from early medieval Europe, anthropologists are not forced to rely on mere speculation when attempting to define what motivated these societies.

The Mixtecs

The Mixtecs, who moved into what is now Oaxaca, the area

previously dominated by Monte Albán and the Zapotecs, were the most cultured of the new arrivals. Although not adverse to warfare, they deliberately intermarried with the Zapotecs, forming a new synthetic culture. They became skilled metallurgists, known for their jewelry, and kept careful historical records adorned with colorful codices on animal skins.

The Mixtecs carefully avoided the deserted Monte Albán, honoring its sacred character, and established Mitla as the center of the new hybrid society. The vibrancy of the Zapotec-Mixtec world no doubt saved the Valley of Oaxaca from the worst of the violence occasioned by new invasions.

The Toltecs

The Toltecs, who arrived in Central Mexico about A.D. 900, were the dominant force throughout most of Mexico for the next two centuries. Although the Toltecs themselves never accounted for more than a minority of the population, they imposed their values and religious beliefs on a vast area extending from north of the present city of Querétaro southwards into the Yucatán.

The Toltecs were governed by a military elite who demanded personal tribute from all whom they conquered. Like the knights of medieval Europe, members of this elite were also constantly at war with each other, competing for hegemony and the fruits of conquest. The history of the Toltec dynasties is a dreary story of assassination, betrayal, and violence. Religion, it seems, was less of a motivating force than it was a device to intimidate victims.

In the midst of this, however, appeared a noble warrior by the name of Topiltzin, a man of high ideals, who vanquished his enemies and seized control of the Toltec world around A.D. 950. He

Toltec soldier figures at Tula. At one time, row after row of these soldiers stood on the platform.

sought to impose a rule of peace and justice, and established Tula as the capital of his enlightened state. (His story is not unlike the legend of King Arthur which dates from the same time.)

Topiltzin was a follower of the ancient god Quetzalcoatl, the Plumed Serpent and a major deity throughout Mexico in the Classic Period. Topiltzin sought to impose the principles advocated by Quetzalcoatl on the Toltecs. At this point, history blends with mythology, as Topiltzin takes on the name of Quetzalcoatl, rules in his name, and indeed assumes the characteristics of that god. Topiltzin-Quetzalcoatl taught his people how to grow corn, and introduced them to writing and the calendar. He discouraged worship of other gods—some would claim he introduced monotheism—and taught charity and tolerance. In place of human sacrifice, a dominant part of Toltec belief, Topiltzin-Quetzalcoatl demanded only symbolic sacrifices of birds, grains, and insects.

Although Topiltzin-Quetzalcoatl had many devoted followers, he also made many enemies. Warrior lords despised his message of peace, and priests of more traditional deities were determined to restore human sacrifice and the religion of fear that accompanied it. His enemies eventually succeeded in driving Topiltzin-Quetzalcoatl from Tula, and immediately undid his reforms. Topiltzin-Quetzalcoatl and his followers wandered first to Cholula, then to the land of the Maya. Finally, disgusted with their rejection of his message, he disappeared to the East across the sea, promising one day to return in the year Ce Acatl, one of the years in the fifty-two year cycle. As the legend matured, Topiltzin-Quetzalcoatl was described as light-complexioned and heavily bearded.

The legend of Topiltzin-Quetzalcoatl, which originated with a real historical figure, is of interest on several levels. It represents a classic struggle between good and evil. It is also a story of the clash of cultures in which the traditional mythology of the Toltecs confronts a gentler world view of the dying culture of Teotihuacan. Finally, the legend assumed enormous significance at the time of the Spanish conquest. Moctezuma's reluctance to confront the Spaniards directly sprung from his belief that Cortés was the returning Topiltzin-Quetzalcoatl.

In any event, the Toltec warrior elite continued its rule of conquest and exploitation for another two centuries. Their influence began to wane in the middle of the twelfth century, their subjects undoubtedly tiring of war and sacrifice. Once again, the northern frontier was open to new conquests. Tula itself was abandoned and its remnants laid to waste.

The Aztecs

The last, and most awesome, of the pre-Columbian cultures of Mexico was that of the Aztecs, or Mexica as they called themselves. In a few short centuries they carved a vast empire out of central Mexico, and introduced a level of prosperity seldom before experienced. Their political and social organization was more enlightened than that of contemporary Europeans. Yet their religious practices, with emphasis on enormous numbers of human sacrifices, were among the most grisly encountered in the Western Hemisphere.

The Valley of Mexico, or Anáhuac, as it was known to the Indians, had long been a cultural crossroads. Its lakes and rich farmland made it attractive to migrants from the arid north. Over the course of many years, cities arose on the shores of the lakes. Peace existed, however, only when the region was dominated by a single power such as with Teotihuacan, then Tula. With the decline of

Tula, violence returned, intensified by the arrival of new, less-civilized tribes from the north. Small city-states declared war on each other even as they resisted the incursions of outsiders. The Valley of Mexico was already suffering from a enduring problem: overpopulation.

The Aztecs arrived in the region around 1250, having wandered for many years from their original homeland in the present state of Nayarit on the northeast coast of the Gulf of California. To the more sophisticated residents of the Valley, the Aztecs were one more tribe of barbarians—treacherous, crude, and violent. Like new arrivals anywhere, they were forced to eke out an existence on land that no one else wanted. However, the warring city-states also recognized the Aztecs' fighting skills, and occasionally hired them as mercenaries.

For their part, the Aztecs seemed determined to flaunt vulgarity. On one occasion, when they were hired as mercenaries by Culhuacán, they not only fought with great gusto, but demonstrated their success to Coxcox, the Culhuacán monarch, with a gift of eight thousand ears. Now participants in the internecine politics of the region, they requested Coxcox to let his daughter become a princess of the Aztecs. Coxcox agreed, and handed over his daughter. The Aztecs, in turn, immediately sacrificed the princess. At a victory banquet soon afterwards Coxcox was greeted with the gruesome sight of dancers wearing the skin of his daughter.

Ostracized once again, the Aztecs were forced to confine themselves to a small uninhabited island in Lake Texcoco. Here, about 1330, they began construction of their great capital, Tenochtitlán. Within a few years they had made alliances with neighboring cities, and the remarkable growth of the Aztec empire was underway.

The Aztecs were a messianic people who believed themselves

chosen by their god Huitzilopochtli, the Hummingbird, god of war and god of the sun. Huitzilopochtli demanded that his sovereignty be extended over all people, and he tolerated no compromise. He required of the Aztecs a constant diet of human blood to ensure his loyalty and support. Once ensconced in Tenochtitlán, the Aztecs rewrote their history to become one long success story. In the revised version, Huitzilopochtli himself chose the location for the Aztec capital with a sign, an eagle perched on a rock devouring a serpent. Today, this image remains the national emblem of Mexico, found in the center of every Mexican flag.

The Aztec empire grew rapidly during the fifteenth century, expanding from the Gulf of Mexico to the Pacific, and south to Oaxaca. Warfare became an end in itself, for it provided a constant flow of victims for human sacrifice. The warrior became the Aztec ideal; only warriors killed in battle or sacrificed for the gods enjoyed an afterlife, as did women who died giving birth to warriors. With success, the frequency and number of sacrificial victims increased; after all, success demonstrated its efficacy. In 1487, some twenty thousand victims were sacrificed to celebrate the opening of a new temple to Huitzilopochtli, and some had to wait their turn in the hot sun for days. When new opportunities for conquest were lacking, the Aztecs staged so-called Flower Wars, fake wars between Tenochtitlán and its tributary cities, to produce victims to keep Huitzilopochtli satisfied. The rulers of both parties to the conflict were invited to witness the sacrifices from behind a screen.

Despite their bloodthirsty nature, the Aztecs brought to central Mexico an age of peace and prosperity. Trade flourished as commercial routes became safe and merchants sold products throughout Mexico. The empire itself was a loose confederation of tributary states: as long as conquered cities supplied Tenochtitlán with booty and sacrificial victims, they were allowed to govern themselves. In a grisly way, the Aztecs brought law and order to the warring societies of their empire; human sacrifice replaced the battlefield.

The world of the Aztecs was a sophisticated one that combined Aztec discipline with the achievements of predecessors. Society was an aristocracy of merit. Although the same families dominated the highest levels of the government, military, and priesthood, individuals could not assume an important post until they had proven themselves in battle and demonstrated virtue and wisdom. Young men from the lower social classes could achieve greatness through extraordinary accomplishment, but for most members of society the social order was fixed. A landed nobility owned much of the best land, supported by both free peasants and slaves. Social class was not, in fact, related to ethnic origin; important families in conquered territories were welcomed into the Aztec nobility.

Aztec society was a puritanical one. Although men could take several wives and as many mistresses as they could afford, adultery (even the thought of it) was a serious crime. Public drunkenness was seriously condemned, except among the elderly. Between men, honor was important; punishments were designed to incur public scorn. Men were expected to be unflinching in the face of danger, and able to withstand pain. Physical prowess was valued. Women were expected to be modest and unassertive, their world restricted to the household. Children were cherished, but taught to respect discipline and the authority of elders.

Government was complex, bureaucratic, and comprehensive. The state assumed responsibility for housing, water, and other public services for all. Aztec society was unique in its time for mandating compulsory education for everyone. Sons of the nobility were versed in theology and history as well as in the skills of warriors. Those from the lower classes learned trades. Girls were taught household tasks. The Aztecs also developed a complex legal system with written laws and courts of law. Punishments were severe and often included death, although convicted criminals were never sacrificed to the gods.

When Moctezuma II assumed the throne in 1504, the empire was at its zenith. Moctezuma carried the traditional theology to a new height, claiming himself to be a god through the intervention of Huitzilopochtli. He was a true believer, not only in himself, but in the accumulated beliefs of centuries. As the end of the fifty-two year cycle approached in 1519, he looked for signs that would indicate whether the world would again be renewed. Human sacrifices increased to forestall disaster. Ominous signs appeared, from the stars in the heavens to food shortages and an increase in alcoholism on earth. Yet, the most threatening of all were rumored sightings of strange beings on the Gulf Coast who bore a remarkable resemblance to the once-exiled Quetzalcoatl.

Moctezuma II.

COLONIAL MEXICO

Mexico, or New Spain as it was known, was a colony of Spain for three centuries, more than one hundred years longer than it has now been an independent country. The institutions and values of the colonial era are deeply entrenched in Mexican society. Indeed, from its architecture to family life, colonial Mexico endures to a far greater extent than colonial English America influences contemporary North America. Even the ethnic character of Mexico has scarcely changed, for Mexico has experienced little immigration since achieving independence in 1822.

Conquest

God! Gold! Glory! These were the cries that in 1519 motivated some 550 Spaniards, accompanied by a few Indians and blacks, to leave the relative security of Cuba to seek greater wealth on the American mainland. The story of the conquest of Mexico is a fascinating one, deserving of some detail, and one that illustrates the similarities and differences between the two cultures that are today Mexico.

The conquest also possesses enormous symbolic value. For the first time, Native Americans and Spanish Europeans confronted each other, ultimately to fuse into Mexicans. Thus, in a sense, the conquest represents the birth of the Mexican people.

Twenty-five years after Columbus arrived in America, the Spaniards were frustrated. Their conquests of Hispaniola, Cuba, Puerto Rico, and Jamaica had yielded little in the way of wealth. Disease and overwork were destroying the Indian population. The American mainland beckoned, enhanced by legends of fabulous civilizations and incalculable wealth.

The leader of the expedition that left Havana in 1519 was Hernán Cortés, who had arrived in the New World in 1504 at the age of nineteen. Already in his short life he had studied law, fought with the Spanish army in Italy, and had almost killed himself climbing out of his mistress' bedroom window in an escape from her angry husband. Once in Cuba, he had quickly established himself as a prosperous rancher and a respected associate of the governor, Diego Velázquez.

The expedition consisted of eleven small vessels, some dozen horses, and small cannon. The men were to receive no pay beyond a share of whatever booty they won. Because of a last-minute dispute with Governor Velázquez, the expedition left Cuba illegally. Landing first on the island of Cozumel, the Spaniards slowly made their way around the Yucatán Peninsula to the north, engaging in several minor battles and acquiring information as they went about the wealth in the interior.

At the site of present-day Vera Cruz, Cortés founded a town, a legal act designed to solidify his position with the Crown. He also burned all his vessels, a particularly daring move, in order to prevent any second thoughts on the part of his men.

A crucial event that contributed not only to the Spaniards' eventual success but also to the rich symbolism of conquest that has plagued Mexicans ever since, occurred on the coast of the present state of Tabasco. There a chieftain, seeking to win the good will of the Spaniards, offered Cortés several Indian maidens as a gift. One of these, baptized Marina, became Cortés' mistress and confident, and later bore him a son. Doña Marina, as she became known, had been raised in the north and sold by merchants to a Maya tribe. As

Hernán Cortés.

a result, she was fluent in both the Maya tongue and in Náhuatl, the language of the Aztecs. Apparently a gifted linguist, she quickly learned Spanish as well. Doña Marina became invaluable as an interpreter for Cortés.

Meanwhile, Cortés played a war of nerves with Moctezuma, who already had been alerted to the Spanish presence. The two leaders sent each other messages of good will, Moctezuma urging the Spaniards to leave, Cortés humbly insisting on the opportunity to meet the renowned emperor. Cortés also sowed confusion in the mind of Moctezuma, first by encouraging local tribes to arrest Aztec tribute collectors, then by secretly releasing them. Thus, he managed to befriend the local Indians as their liberator while simultaneously appearing to be a supporter of Aztec sovereignty.

In August 1519, Cortés began the trek into the interior, leaving some one hundred men behind in Vera Cruz. He was accompanied by Doña Marina and over a thousand Indian carriers provided by the towns he had befriended on the coast. The two-hundred mile journey toward Tenochtitlán itself was a challenge, first passing through the steamy jungle, then across frigid mountains. (The Spaniards adapted to the heat by exchanging their heavy armor for the lighter, closely-woven cloth used by Indian warriors.) His native guides served him well; his route through the modern cities of Jalapa, Tlaxcala, and Puebla is today the principal highway and rail route from Vera Cruz to Mexico City.

Some Indian towns welcomed Cortés with gifts and promises of support, as Moctezuma had directed. Others resisted. Everywhere the Spanish appeared impregnable, skillfully combining their superior fighting skills with psychological warfare. The Indians were especially fearful of the Spaniards' massive horses and dogs, animals they had never seen before. For awhile the Spaniards were able to maintain the myth that horses were immortal by secretly burying any horses injured in combat. Moctezuma became increasingly fearful of the mysterious visitors, who appeared to be invincible, and ordered a new wave of human sacrifices. He even offered annual tribute to Cortés and his monarch if the Spaniards would withdraw. Such offers only increased the greed of the Spaniards, who nevertheless recognized their tenuous position, surrounded as they were by hundreds of thousands of Indians.

The turning point came with the Tlaxcalans, sworn enemies of the Aztecs. After several skirmishes, which the Spaniards won, the Tlaxcalans agreed to join the Spaniards in their crusade against the Aztecs. The Spanish invasion had become a civil war, with victims of Aztec oppression fighting alongside the invaders. The empire built on fear was falling victim to its own tyranny.

The Tlaxcalans remained a privileged people throughout the colonial period, immune from the tribute required of other Native Americans. (Modern nationalist thought views them as traitors.) At the time, of course, the Tlaxcalans had no concept of an apocalyptic struggle between European and Native American, between Christianity and indigenous religion. They simply chose to align themselves with the powerful visitors in their age-old fight against the Aztecs.

Moctezuma feared the Spanish-Tlaxcalan alliance, and sent word that Cortés should proceed to the holy city of Cholula, adjacent to the present city of Puebla, where he planned a final confrontation. The Cholulans initially welcomed the Spaniards with flowers and gifts, then seemed to ignore them. While the Spaniards took respite from the long march, the Cholulans secretly planned an attack from hidden fortifications surrounding the city.

The evening before the Indian counterattack was scheduled to begin, Doña Marina caught word of it. She immediately informed Cortés, who summoned the Cholulan leaders to his tent to confront them with their duplicity. He refused to accept their protestations that they were acting on the orders of Moctezuma, once again sowing confusion in the Aztec capital since Moctezuma was still undecided whether the Spaniards were friends or enemies. Meanwhile, Cortés was determined to teach the Cholulans—and Moctezuma—a lesson. He had his men surround the main plaza and slaughter all men, women, and children inside. In the battle that followed, more than six thousand Indians died. Cortés' Indian allies then sacked the city.

With the failure of the Cholulan conspiracy Moctezuma, still uncertain whether the visitors were gods or men, became resigned to their entering Tenochtitlán, only sixty miles from Cholula across one last range of mountains. To the relief of the Spaniards, he informed them that he would welcome them into his capital, eliminating their fear that they would have to fight their way in.

On November 8, 1519, the Spaniards, accompanied by their Indian allies, crossed the pass between the two volcanoes overlooking Tenochtitlán. What awe they must have experienced at the sight of the immense city on Lake Texcoco, larger than any they had known in Spain and resplendent with palaces, markets, and shrines. For the first time they fully realized the wealth and power they encountered, and their incredible luck in reaching this point without having had to directly confront the armed might of the Aztecs.

The Spaniards ceremoniously—and cautiously—crossed the main causeway under the gaze of curious residents. Once in the city, Cortés and Moctezuma finally confronted each other, exchanging gifts and signs of respect. Moctezuma, taking no chances at this point, welcomed Cortés as Quetzalcoatl, and offered his guests hospitality at one of his palaces. The Spaniards were now the guests of the people they hoped to conquer—and their prisoners as well. For the next few days, the Spaniards behaved like tourists, both amazed at the luxury and wealth of the city and repulsed by the racks of skulls and the priests with dried blood in their hair.

Hearing rumors from his Tlaxcalan allies that the Aztecs were planning to massacre the Spaniards, Cortés again resorted to psychological warfare. He seized the person of Moctezuma, a frequent visitor to the guest palace, and told him he would remain a prisoner of the Spaniards. Moctezuma, for his part, resigned himself to this humiliation, apparently still convinced that he was acquiescing to the will of gods more powerful than himself. The Spaniards treated him well, and allowed him to continue to administer his empire under their watchful eyes. Meanwhile, the Spaniards insisted on an end to human sacrifice, and had a statue of the Virgin installed atop the high pyramid in place of the Aztec idols. Moctezuma by now must have reluctantly acknowledged to himself that he had been betrayed. Other less docile religious and military leaders, however, were determined to drive out the invaders.

Moctezuma's fortunes improved with word that a rival Spanish force from Cuban Governor Velázquez had arrived on the coast. It appeared that the Spaniards might drive each other out of Mexico. Cortés divided his force and quickly marched to the coast where, in a surprise attack, he defeated the newcomers and added one hundred horses and some eight hundred men to his forces. He left three hundred men behind in Tenochtitlán under the leadership of the impetuous Pedro de Alvarado.

While Cortés was still on the coast, the Aztecs in Tenochtitlán prepared to celebrate their annual religious celebration, minus the traditional human sacrifice. Alvarado mistook the preparations as a threat, and had his men surround the main square. At a given signal, they attacked the worshipers, killing several hundred. The Aztecs were furious, and forced the Spaniards back into their guest palace, which they quickly fortified against attack. The Spaniards were now prisoners in their own palace, Alvarado having made the fatal mistake of taking on an entire population instead of trying to manipulate its leaders.

Cortés, hearing the news, rushed back to the capital hoping for a miracle. For several days the Spaniards repulsed waves of attackers, but realized they could not hold out much longer. As a last resort, Cortés once again turned to Moctezuma to plead with his people. Moctezuma climbed onto the roof, and was immediately hit with a stone, whether deliberately or by accident it shall never be known for sure. He died three days later. (Aztec sources claimed the Spaniards killed Moctezuma.)

Moctezuma today is not viewed as a heroic figure. His caution, fed by religious convictions, had kept him from driving out the Spaniards when he still had a chance. He had capitulated to the Spaniards each time, always hoping he would be able to win control of the situation in the future. He never succeeded. Moctezuma was succeeded by his young nephew, Cuauhtémoc, a man of action who held no doubts about the intentions of the Spaniards. Cortés realized his position was untenable, and planned a retreat. Unable to fight their way out of Tenochtitlán in daylight, the Spaniards planned to secretly withdraw under cover of darkness. On the evening of July 1, dubbed the noche triste in the mythology, the Spaniards quietly withdrew, crossing the two-mile-long Tacuba causeway to the mainland. They were heard, however, and the

Aztecs attacked en masse. The Spaniards, weighted down with booty, fought desperately. Many fell into the lake and drowned, immediately sinking to the bottom under the weight of their stolen gold. Alvarado is reputed to have made a superhuman leap across water to safety. (Today the street, Puente de Alvarado, or Alvarado's bridge, marks the spot.) Almost five hundred Spaniards and several thousand Indian allies perished. The dream of taking the Aztec capital by deceit had failed.

Cortés and his men retreated to Tlaxcala to regroup. Fortunately, his Indian allies feared Aztec retribution more than the Spaniards; if they had not, all would have been lost. For the next year, both sides prepared for total warfare, with none of the diplomatic niceties that had accompanied the first entrance into Tenochtitlán.

A year later, the Spaniards returned to the Valley of Mexico, setting up camp in Texcoco. With their Indian allies they blockaded the city, preventing the entrance of food and reinforcements. The Aztecs suffered an additional blow with the outbreak of a smallpox epidemic, apparently the result of the diseases inadvertently introduced into Tenochtitlán during the Spanish stay there. Meanwhile, additional well-armed Spaniards arrived from Cuba, and their Indian allies grew in number. Cortés had eleven wooden vessels constructed for a naval attack.

The final assault on Tenochtitlán began in May 1521 with a naval assault. The Spaniards quickly gained control of the lake, the causeways connecting the capital with the mainland, and the aqueducts, thereby depriving the Aztecs of food and water. Actual seizure of the city proved more difficult, as the defenders resorted to block-by-block fighting. Both sides fought bravely, though the final outcome was never in doubt. The Aztecs sacrificed new vic-

Cortés and his men battle the Aztecs.

tims to Huitzilopochtli, including some Spanish prisoners, an act which only spurred the Spaniards to greater efforts. The Spaniards destroyed buildings and temples as they progressed, depriving the defenders of fortifications from which to counterattack. Finally, on August 13, 1521, Tenochtitlán fell. Cuauhtémoc was captured and executed. The city was little more than a pile of rubble. The mighty empire of the Aztecs had fallen to some one thousand Europeans.

For both Aztec and Spaniard, the final Spanish victory was not only a human victory but a victory of the Christian God worshiped by the Spaniards over Aztec deities. Indeed, the war of the conquest was a war between gods as well as between men.

For two hundred years, the Aztec god of war, Huitzilopochtli, had led his followers to victory in return for the sacrifice of their victims. The Aztecs were a chosen people; their success was evidence of their special place in the cosmos. Yet, success was not inevitable. In the years immediately preceding the arrival of the Spaniards, the heavens were filled with foreboding signs. Moctezuma, the Aztec emperor, feared the end was near even before the Spaniards arrived. The Spaniards were agents of the inevitable. The defeat of the Aztec empire represented the defeat of Huitzilopochtli by the god of the conquerors.

To be sure, the Aztecs did all in their power to strengthen Huitzilopochtli. During the siege of Tenochtitlán, thousands of victims—including Spanish prisoners—were sacrificed as a last ditch effort. But Huitzilopochtli either did not hear, or was powerless to help. Thus, the ready acceptance of Christianity by the native population was as much their recognition of reality, the supremacy of the Christian God, as it was the result of effective proselytizing by the Spaniards.

The Spanish conquistadors, in turn, attributed their success to the Catholic God and His saints. They were engaged in a religious crusade, a holy war designed to stamp out idolatry and to bring Christianity to the natives of the New World. Their victory affirmed the nobility of their crusade. Christianity not only legitimized the conquest, it ennobled it.

The association of conquest with a holy war was not a novel idea to sixteenth-century Spaniards. The legends with which young men grew up told of the earlier crusades of the Reconquest, when Christians regained the Iberian Peninsula from the Moslem Moors. Granada, the last Moslem holdout, had only been reconquered in 1492, the year Columbus discovered America.

Religion, then, was more than a mere rationalization for conquest. This does not mean, of course, that every Spaniard was deeply religious, or much less behaved in a Christian manner. The thinking was more complex. The enterprise of conquest was a noble one; Spain was entrusted with a righteous mission, and each individual Spaniard participated in this mission. At the same time, individual Spaniards did not assume individual responsibilities to convert the Indians, or even to treat them well. Rather, conquest provided the opportunity for adventure and self-aggrandizement in a manner blessed by the Church. In other words, the enterprise was noble even though the motives of individuals were selfish.

Today one is hard-pressed to find a statue or memorial to Cortés, the foreigner who vanquished the people of Mexico. Moctezuma has become a pathetic figure, a victim of his own superstition. Only Cuauhtémoc remains a hero, admired for his courage. His statue stands at the geographical center of Mexico City.

Still, it is impossible not to admire the cleverness of Hernán Cortés. His insight into the society he hoped to defeat, regarding its fears and the dread in which it was held by its victims, served him well. He came close to defeating a vast empire without extensive bloodshed. Once Tenochtitlán fell, he proved himself a statesman of considerable wisdom as well. He quickly set about to rebuild the city, organize a government, convert the Indians to Christianity, and revive the shattered economy by importing European animals and plants. Ironically, he was least successful in controlling the thousands of Spaniards who flocked to Mexico once word of the conquest spread. His efforts to moderate the exploitation of the Indians failed. He, himself, though richly rewarded in land and Indians, soon found himself deprived of any role in the new government, and lived out his days a frustrated and disappointed man.

Lastly, we must remember that the conquest of Mexico was not only a European victory over Native Americans, but also a civil war among the indigenous inhabitants. Cortés could not have succeeded without his thousands of Indian allies; for, to many subject peoples of the Aztec empire, the Spanish war of conquest was at first a war of liberation.

New Spain

Once Tenochtitlán had been defeated, the conquerors moved quickly to create in America a New Spain, the official designation for Mexico during the next three hundred years. The word "new," however, had a more limited connotation than it would have for the English in New England. For the English, "new" meant a land that was a new creation, something very different from "old England." The Spanish, on the other hand, did not aim to create something different—they had no quarrel with the "old" Spain— but rather wished to recreate Spain in the New World. Indeed, both the climate and the terrain of Mexico were not unlike those of Spain.

The Spaniards benefitted from the highly centralized nature of the Aztec state. Aided by its tribute records, Cortés assigned his men individual towns from which to exact tribute and Indian labor, the first ones being independent towns around the lake—Coyoacán, Atzcapotzalco, Tlatelolco—which would serve as a base from which to rebuild Mexico City.

Cortés then sent expeditions out in all directions, south to Oaxaca and Chiapas, west to Michoacán and the Pacific, and southeast to the Yucatán. Outside the areas once controlled by the Aztecs there was considerable resistance, and considerable excesses committed on the part of the Spaniards. In present-day Michoacán, the conquest of the Tarascans by Niño de Guzmán, a competitor of Cortés, was particularly brutal. He burned villages, tortured captured chiefs, and enslaved entire communities.

The economic foundation of New Spain was established with the discovery of rich deposits of silver near the contemporary cities of Zacatecas, Guanajuato, and San Luis Potosí, northwest of the capital. Silver became Mexico's principal export throughout the colonial period. It was silver, along with the exploitation of native labor, that financed the growth of Mexico, its immense bureaucracies of church and state, and the wars of the Spanish monarchy in Europe. Mexican silver also contributed to one hundred years of inflation throughout most of Western Europe.

The dream of encountering other Tenochtitláns, reinforced by traditional legends, inspired expeditions to the north which lasted for years. The most ambitious was that of Francisco Vázquez de Coronado. Coronado's expedition, searching for the legendary Seven Cities of Gold, explored present-day New Mexico, Arizona, Colorado, and Kansas. One can readily imagine Native Americans encouraging the Spaniards to press on further in their quest rather than to settle in their own territories. The wild horses encountered centuries later by Americans moving west were probably descendants of animals left behind by Coronado.

By the end of the sixteenth century, the Spaniards had explored all of contemporary Mexico and much of the American Southwest and Guatemala. The core of New Spain extended from the Gulf of Mexico to the Pacific, to Zacatecas and San Luis Potosí in the north, and to Oaxaca and the Yucatán in the south. Beyond to the north was the frontier, sparsely settled, dotted with an occasional mission or military outpost (*presidio*). Monterrey, today a bustling industrial center, was a sleepy frontier town.

The pattern of settlement reflected Spanish ambitions. Unlike the English a century later, the Spanish had little use for unoccupied land. (Spain itself was sparsely populated.) Instead, it was a settled Native American population that made an area attractive. It would have been inconceivable to drive Indians away. The Spanish came not to settle land but to conquer and rule an indigenous population. European settlement of New Spain stopped where a large settled Indian population stopped. The continuous land which is today the United States, of which the colonists were well aware, was of little interest; its native population was too sparse, too unsettled, and too warlike.

Like most Mediterranean peoples, the Spanish associated civilization with cities. Cities were an integral part of the colonizing enterprise, and building cities was the first step everywhere to establishing a Spanish presence. Virtually all of the cities of central Mexico were founded within a generation of the conquest.

Some cities were established to serve specific needs, such as mining centers or garrisons. More frequently, however, the Spaniards constructed their cities on the ruins of Indian cities, as they had first done in the capital. Often they used the very stones of the destroyed Indian temples to construct cathedrals and government buildings.

Colonial Spanish American cities also represent one of the earliest western attempts at urban planning. New World cities were carefully designed to resemble cities in Spain. With their massive stone structures they were designed to last (they have!), and to provide their more fortunate inhabitants with all the amenities of a civilized life. Most wealthy families maintained a city home as well as a residence close to their *hacienda* or mining enterprise.

Every city had a central square, or *zócalo*, for public events and a place for vendors to display their crafts. Around the square were symbols of church and state: a cathedral and government buildings. Branching out from the square, terrain permitting, were straight, parallel streets that crossed at right angles. In larger cities, smaller squares might be located at certain intervals. Adjacent to the main square were the mansions of the rich. Each craft had its designated block so that all jewelers or carpenters, for example, were located together. Further away from the city center were the more modest dwellings of workers. City governments maintained public fountains for water, and paid night watchmen to ward off crime. The downtown areas of most cities founded during the colonial period have changed little since.

An Ecological Revolution

The conquest of the New World not only brought Americans and Europeans into contact, but also increased the plants, animals, and diseases available to both peoples; for, until the Spanish arrived in America, the two ecological environments had not had contact for thousands of years.

Native American food was the food North Americans associate with Mexico today: corn and corn meal, beans, peppers, and tomatoes, none of which existed in Europe before Columbus. (Europeans still use the Indian term maize for what we know as corn; in England, "corn" is a generic term for all grains.) Chocolate, a luxury, was grown in the South of Mexico. And Native Americans used the juice of the maguey plant—the cactus frequently used to mark the border of a field—for pulque, a mild, milky alcoholic beverage. (When distilled, it becomes tequila.) The Spaniards brought to Native Americans domesticated animals such as cattle, horses, pigs, and chickens, and grains such as wheat, oats, and rice, and a variety of vegetables. During the colonial period, each culture continued to consume its traditional fare; even in the twentieth century, anthropologists use eating habits, especially wheat bread or tortillas, as one method of measuring the degree to which Indians have been assimilated.

This so-called Columbian exchange also contributed to much human misery. The Europeans brought with them smallpox, measles, pneumonia, and typhoid. The Indians, having no resistance to these diseases, perished by the tens of thousands during the early decades of colonization. Americans, in turn, gave Europe syphilis, or at least a particular virulent strain of that malady, an especially appropriate gift in light of the widespread rape that accompanied the conquest.

Colonial Mexico

The Spaniards sought to conquer people, not to occupy land. Many aspired to establish themselves as wealthy landowners, supported by hundreds of Indian peasants. Others came for quick wealth and the adventure of warfare. (Many early conquistadors seemed unable to settle down; as soon as one expedition was successfully concluded, they went off on another.) Still others, a minority, came to America to convert Native Americans to Christianity. For most, however, the motives were mixed; Spaniards saw no contradiction in enriching themselves while spreading the word of God. Thus, the missionary endeavor was not a rationalization, but an integral part of the colonizing enterprise.

Within a generation of the conquest, the Spaniards had defined for themselves the nature of the society they would create. Since the Indians supplied essential labor, they were not driven to the frontier. Since conversion to Christianity was an integral part of the endeavor, they could not be enslaved. Rather, the Indians became the dependent labor class, not unlike the peasant class of Europe. They also became Catholics.

The Spaniards initially envisioned what they dubbed "two republics," two distinct societies of Spaniards and Indians living side by side, each observing their own customs and speaking their own languages. They established separate educational systems, separate law courts, and distinct systems of local government. They did not set out deliberately to destroy indigenous culture beyond converting it to Christianity.

Whatever merit lay in the concept, however, was frustrated by reality. Aggressive conversion to Christianity, combined with a determination to exterminate all remnants of indigenous religious practice, destroyed the integrity of Indian culture. Labor requirements forced Indians into the European economy in a subordinate, dependent role with no opportunity to participate as equals. Hence, what in theory was an attempt to preserve aspects of indigenous culture became in fact a kind of apartheid whose primary purpose was to subordinate the Indians for the benefit of Europeans. The labor demands created by the development of silver mines destroyed even the pretense of toleration. Labor drafts forced Indians to leave their villages for long periods; some continued to work in mines for pay because they had little to go back to.

For the first generation after the conquest, the dominant institution of Spanish-Indian relations was the *encomienda*, a uniquely Spanish institution that relied on a non-existent altruism among the conquistadors and thus resulted in a blank check for exploitation. Indian villages were entrusted to Spaniards, who were obliged to care for physical needs and oversee conversion to Christianity. In return, the Spaniards could demand tribute and compel labor. The *encomienda*, when combined with land grants, quickly became a New World form of feudalism. Wealthy landowners, all but immune from government control, became petty tyrants on their lands. The Indian population, helpless to resist, came to depend on the landowner, the *patrón*, for its very survival.

Despite the Spanish demand for Indian labor, the first century of colonization witnessed the virtual genocide of the indigenous population. By 1650 the indigenous population of central Mexico had declined from some 20 million at the time of the conquest to only 1 million. Many had died from the wars of conquest and from overwork, especially in the mining areas. Some, no doubt seeing their culture destroyed, their gods defeated, and themselves destined to a life of slavery, lost the will to live. The vast majority, however, succumbed to disease. Frequent plagues devastated the indigenous population, already weakened by conquest, exploitation, and malnutrition.

The decline in population led in turn to a new institution, the *hacienda*, that would dominate rural Mexico until the beginning of the twentieth century. The *hacienda* was an enormous landholding, or *latifundio*, with a large resident Indian population. The peasants worked for the landholder; in return, they were given use of a small plot of land. It was a classic patron-client relationship: the peasants were completely dependent on the good will of the landowner, and the landowner, at best, cared for his dependents in a most patronizing manner. He might provide religious services, occasional fiestas, even education for a bright Indian lad. In its classic form, the *hacienda* had more land and labor than it needed; its objective was to provide a secure income for its owner, not necessarily to maximize profits. *Hacienda* Indians were relatively lucky, given the alternatives of unemployment, vagrancy, and migrant labor. Ultimately, the *hacienda* survived because it offered dependent peasants as well as landowners at least minimal security—at vastly different levels, obviously—in a world in which survival was constantly at risk.

Despite the enduring significance of the Spanish-Indian relationships in the countryside through most of Mexican history, Mexico has neither preserved nor restored remnants of the traditional *hacienda*. Contemporary thinking does not romanticize Mexico's feudal past in the same manner as does the American South. Many *haciendas* were destroyed during the 1910 Revolution; those that remain value their privacy.

More recently, the tourist industry has discovered North

Peasant at work on a hacienda.

Hacienda *in southern Mexico—part home, part church, part fortress.*

America's fascination with the luxury of times past, and has attempted to duplicate the style of Spanish aristocrats. For many, one favorite is Las Mañanitas in Cuernavaca. This gourmet taste of the good life should be balanced with a visit to Cortés' palace just off the main square, where murals by Diego Rivera graphically represent the exploitation of the Indians that made such wealth possible.

Rural Indian villages remain, of course; their physical appearance has not changed a great deal other than that concrete has replaced adobe, and now there are the ubiquitous Coca-Cola signs. One can also appreciate the enormous gap that divides rural poverty from modern Mexico, and better understand the desperation that drives so many to seek a better life in large cities or in the United States.

Colonial Institutions

Power in colonial Mexico was a paradox. In theory, the king of Spain held all power. He ruled New Spain through a rigid hierarchy of appointed officials who were in no way accountable to those they governed. Yet, in practice, government was largely ineffective, so that in fact the elite of Spanish America were far more free of government regulation than their counterparts in English America. In other words, in English America colonists participated in government, and government mattered. In Spanish America, colonists had little opportunity to participate, but government was easy to ignore.

Every school child in America, for example, has heard about the stamp tax imposed by the British. Americans resented the tax, and organized protests and boycotts until Parliament withdrew it. Such a series of events is hard to imagine in colonial Mexico. If Spain had passed legislation the colonists resented, they would have simply ignored it. And this is what often happened. (New Spain did have a stamp tax, incidentally, but it caused little controversy.)

This basic dichotomy between formal power and de facto power has continued to dominate Mexico to the present. Mexicans recognize this; unlike their counterparts to the north, they look upon power and its use as something much broader than the institutions of government.

To be sure, Spanish government in America was formidable. Representing the Crown was the viceroy of New Spain, who governed not only what is Mexico today but also the American southwest, Central America down to Panama, and the Spanish islands of the Caribbean. He and his large staff resided in what is today the National Palace in Mexico City. This huge territory was divided into *audiencias*. Mexico itself had two *audiencias*, one in Mexico City and one, the Audiencia of New Galicia, located in Guadalajara. Under the *audiencias* were a bewildering array of *corregidores, alcaldes mayores*, and *gobernadores*. From time to time, Spain also sent *visitadores* to check up on its officials and to recommend changes. At the local level, towns were governed by councils called *cabildos;* only at this level were there occasional elections. Legal decisions could always be appealed to a higher level, even to the king of Spain if the litigator had sufficient funds and patience.

At every level, an official received his appointment from the official above him in the hierarchy, and served at the pleasure of his superior. Office holders were accountable not to the people they governed, but to their superior in the hierarchy.

The system also lacked any concept of checks and balances.

Officials at every level not only administered the law, but also issued decrees and served as judges when the law was violated. Thus, colonial government recognized no distinction between executive, legislative, and judicial functions. This legacy continues today even though the Mexican constitution formally outlines a separate legislature and judiciary. Realistically, the president and state governors rule without restriction from the legislature or courts.

Spanish colonial government was never as effective as its structure suggested. Distances were long, decisions traveled slowly, and legislation was often unrealistic. Indeed, there arose a standard response to decrees from Spain: "I obey, but I do not comply." In other words, "I recognize the authority of the Spanish Crown, but will follow my own best judgment in practice."

Other factors further weakened the effectiveness of government. Many public offices were sold to the highest bidder. Office holders looked upon their positions as investments; they were determined to recover what they had paid to obtain the positions, accumulate funds to pay the inevitable fines for corruption in office, and then retire comfortably. (Every official faced a formal hearing, the *residencia*, at the end of his term. Supposedly a device to discourage corruption, it soon became only another cost of doing business.) Since salaries were low, regional and local office holders looked for extra-legal sources of income. One of the most common forms of abuse was to force Indians to purchase goods that they did not need at outrageous prices.

Often a candidate seeking public office had to borrow the money he needed to buy the position from a wealthy landowner or merchant. As a result, he became more beholden to the local power structure than to the authorities in Mexico City. Powerful families, in turn, became virtual dictators in their own domains, immune from government regulation and the courts. The indigenous population had to depend on the good will of landowners, not government, for its well being. In other words, Spanish colonial government on the regional and local level was little more than an instrument of the landed elite. Public office as a public trust was an alien concept in colonial Mexico.

The legacy of colonial institutions lasted long after independence. Powerful families and commercial interests remained more interested in protecting their immunity from government than in influencing its policies. The line between public and private remained blurred. Government remained the property of those who held office. And the vast majority of Mexicans remained powerless to influence their national destiny.

Religion in Colonial Mexico

Religion dominated life in colonial Mexico. Churches dotted the countryside, and were the cornerstone of every city neighborhood. Church bells marked the time of day; men and women of the clergy were everywhere in public, and were an essential presence at every important political or social occasion. The institutional Catholic Church was in theory an equal partner in government, but, in practice, a virtual tool of the Spanish monarchy, since the Crown appointed all bishops. The Church came to possess huge amounts of wealth in land and mines, and was itself a giant bureaucracy.

New Spain, then, was a Catholic society not because of the piety or virtue of its members, but because of the power of the institutional Church. The symbols of its pervasive power were everywhere, from grand cathedrals with altars covered with gold and silver, to small statues and shrines in the most remote villages. The clergy attracted not only the devout, but also those who sought a prestigious career with a secure income. In most upper class families, at least one son was destined for the priesthood. Unmarried women entered the convent. (Recent research has suggested that the convent was one of the few places in which women could achieve considerable power and control over wealth.)

Not all serious Catholics were content with just an institutional presence, however. Many clergy, particularly representatives of religious orders—Franciscans, Dominicans, Augustinians, and later Jesuits—were determined to bring Christianity to the native population. Initially, efforts were devoted to baptizing as many Indians as possible, and individual priests boasted of having baptized many thousands in a single day. Indians offered little resistance; they were accustomed to accepting the gods of their conquerors, and having water poured over their heads was a modest demand. Once the Indians were nominally Christian, the clergy established schools to educate the new converts in the basics of their faith, and reading and writing. Some schools attempted more, from crafts to Scholastic philosophy.

It was easier to get the Indians to accept Christianity than to give up their old beliefs. Traditionally, the acceptance of new gods did not require turning away from the old; there was room in the cosmos for everyone. For the Spaniards, however, the former idols were not only incompatible with Christianity, but also threatened universal acceptance of Spanish sovereignty. The first bishop of Mexico, Juan de Zumárraga, went to great lengths to uncover small statues of Indian gods buried in caves. Everywhere, the Spaniards destroyed existing shrines and temples, often using the stones to construct churches on the same location.

At the same time, the Spanish clergy did not demand complete conformity. They recognized the distinction between religion and culture, and did not compel potential converts to accept all the rubrics of Spanish culture as part of their Catholicism. Moreover, they encouraged the transition by identifying Catholic saints with indigenous gods, often adapting traditional customs to the worship of a local patron saint. As a result, religion even today embraces many different practices—indeed, different cultures—within the framework of Mexican Catholicism. Spanish Catholicism was very flexible as long as it was sovereign.

Guadalupe

The single most dramatic event in the conversion of the Indian population to Christianity was the appearance of Our Lady of Guadalupe in 1531. The simple charm of the story, whether one is a believer or not, has made Guadalupe the focus of Mexican identity and indigenous pride for four hundred years.

Juan Diego was a humble, devout Indian recently converted to Catholicism. While crossing a barren hill, Tepeyac, on his way to Mass, the Virgin suddenly appeared before him. She told him to go to the bishop, Juan Zumárraga, and tell him that she wanted a church built atop the hill. Two days later, Juan Diego was granted an audience, and gave Zumárraga the message. The bishop was sympathetic, but demanded proof, which Juan Diego relayed back to the Virgin. The Virgin then told Juan to gather the roses growing on top of the hill, where roses had never grown before, and take them to the bishop. Juan complied, gathering them in the blanket he carried, and returned to the bishop. When he opened the blanket to show the bishop, however, the roses had disappeared. Instead, an image of the Virgin, modestly adorned in Indian garb, appeared on his blanket. Zumárraga accepted the evidence, and ordered a church built where the Virgin had requested.

The symbolism of the Virgin image was powerful. It was not the image of a European woman, but rather a dark-complexioned Indian woman with notably Indian features. The message was clear: Christianity was a religion not only for white Europeans, but for all. To the Indians, the Virgin of Guadalupe was one of them, welcoming them into the new faith. To the Spaniards, the Virgin of Guadalupe denied the second-class membership of Indians within Christianity. And to Mexicans of the future, the Virgin of Guadalupe became a national patron.

The location of the apparition was even more compelling. Tepeyac had previously been a site where Indians went to worship Tonantzín, a mother figure in indigenous religious belief that predated the Aztecs. Whether or not by design, the location further promoted the transition from traditional belief to Christianity.

The cult of the Virgin of Guadalupe was a modest one until the eighteenth century, when the apparition was officially recognized by the Catholic Church in Rome. During the war of independence, the image of the Virgin of Guadalupe became the emblem of Mexican independence from Spain, and Native American liberation from the Europeans. (Whites in Mexico City offered prayers to Our Lady of Los Remedios.) Since 1810, Guadalupe has become as much a symbol of Mexican nationalism and social justice as it is a badge of piety.

Utopian Christianity

Some missionaries, particularly the Franciscans, had a far more radical vision of Christianity than simply to bring Native Americans under the Catholic umbrella. Inspired by the humanist thought of the late Renaissance, they viewed America as a God-given opportunity to create a perfect Christian society, far removed from the decadence and corruption of the Old World. The Indians, they were convinced, possessed an innocence Europeans had long since lost. In order to fulfill their vision, Franciscans established missions far beyond the frontiers of European settlement. These missions, whose structures still stand in Texas and California, were designed as self-contained communities in which all property was shared in common. The Indians who settled in the mission received training in agriculture and crafts as well as in Catholic belief and liturgy. Many of the missions were economic as well as religious successes.

Some historians have criticized the missions for treating the Indians like children, and encouraging a docile behavior that made them more vulnerable to later conquest. Nevertheless, one cannot help but admire the missionaries' vision and courage, striking out into the unknown in twos and threes with only their trust in God to sustain them.

Other clergy served as critics of the worst abuses of conquest. Most prominent of these was Bartolomé de Las Casas, a Dominican who questioned not only the manner in which the Indians were forced to become laborers for the Spaniards, but Spain's very right to colonize the New World. He did believe Spain had an obligation to convert the Indians to Catholicism, but without conquest and exploitation. His graphic descriptions of Spanish excesses and cogent arguments were taken seriously back in Spain, where the Crown not only demanded reform but also sponsored a series of debates among Spain's most prominent philosophers on

Bartolomé de Las Casas.

the legitimacy of Spain's presence in the New World. Las Casas eventually became bishop of Chiapas in the south of Mexico.

In Mexico City, Bishop Juan de Zumárraga, himself a Franciscan, also became a staunch defender of the Indians. Formally taking the title Protector of the Indians, he created a custom whereby one day a week was reserved to hearing complaints of Indians against the Spaniards. He also took it upon himself to report to Spain the worst abuses, even to the point of demanding a change in the political leadership. He was successful.

It was no doubt inevitable that neither arguments nor lobbying efforts would succeed in undoing the conquest. Too many, in both Spain and in America, had profited from it. Once the rich deposits of silver were discovered after 1550, excessive concern over the ethics of conquest became a luxury Spain could not afford. However, it was to Spain's credit that at least for a time it took seriously the moral issues associated with the colonization of the New World.

The idealism of the early friars inevitably brought them into conflict with landowners and royal officials. Landowners viewed them as naïve dreamers who did not understand the economic realities of life, and as a dangerous political force that was preventing them access to additional Indian labor. Spanish officials resented the friars' criticisms and their efforts to usurp secular authority. The Church hierarchy, generally more worldly, took offense at their autonomy and self-righteousness.

The Institutional Church

The dominant Church of bishops and secular clergy (those clergy directly under the local bishop and not members of religious orders),

Bishop Juan de Zumárraga.

cathedrals and imposing monasteries, lavish ritual and legalistic bureaucracy, was less troublesome to the establishment of New Spain. It legitimized the status quo by preaching the virtues of humility, resignation to God's will, and obedience to lawful authority.

The Church was also spectacularly wealthy; by the end of the colonial period, it owned over half of the real estate in Mexico either directly or as mortgage holder. (At a time before banks and stock exchanges, the Church was the principal source of capital.) It had received some of its property as endowments from the government, far more as gifts. Income from these holdings paid for larger and more grandiose churches and monasteries, and supported schools, hospitals, and social services. It also provided a comfortable life for successful members of the clergy.

The clergy and the land they controlled were exempt from all taxation, and from the jurisdiction of secular courts in both criminal and civil matters. They jealously protected their legal privileges, or *fueros*. Indeed, the life of the Catholic clergy was so attractive that the Church had difficulty finding positions for all of its members. Parishes were handed out like patronage. Some priests found a sinecure in the employ of a wealthy landowner. Small wonder that the Sunday sermons on a large *hacienda* seldom challenged the status quo.

Ecclesiastical courts had exclusive jurisdiction over questions of morality, including marriage. (Control over marriage had important economic implications, since the legitimacy of a child would affect inheritance.) The Church, not the state, registered births in conjunction with baptism, and buried the dead. Church membership was not a matter of choice but a matter of fact, as unavoidable and automatic as citizenship is today.

The most notorious agency of the Catholic Church was the Inquisition, transported from Spain by Bishop Zumárraga. Its purpose was to enforce religious and political orthodoxy by rooting out heresy in thought and practice, and censoring books and ideas. The Inquisition relied on informants and torture for its investigations, and public *autos de fe*—ceremonial public confessions of guilt followed by punishment—for its authority. Its principal victims were the occasional Protestant (always labeled Lutheran) or Jew, and practitioners of witchcraft and sorcery. Indians were immune from the Inquisition since, it was argued, their childlike Christianity rendered them incapable of conscious heresy.

Like other agencies of state, the Inquisition was never as effective as its image suggests. Non-Catholics with needed skills were frequently protected, even by local governments. Sorcery was never eliminated. Literate Mexicans managed to stay in touch with the latest European authors even though their books were condemned as heretical.

The legacy of colonial Spanish Catholicism, then, was not its absolute control over what people thought and did, but the idea that such control was desirable. Morality, according to this tradition, cannot be left to the individual, who is inclined to selfishness, but must be imposed from above.

Colonial Society

Colonial Mexican society was a multicultural world of Native Americans, Europeans, and African-Americans living in close proximity, yet culturally distinct. At the same time, enormous differences in wealth and status not only separated the three cultures, but also created divisions within the dominant white population.

Even before the conquest, both Indian and Spanish societies contained rigid class distinctions. Sixteenth-century Spain, reflecting the values of late medieval Europe, perpetuated the concept of a society strictly divided according to class and social function. A well-ordered society, it was thought, was one in which everyone knew his or her place (gender divisions were perhaps the most powerful), and in which everyone respected the privileges and obligations that went with one's status. It made sense that one's legal position depended on one's function in society (nobility, profession, ancestry); to assert an abstract equality appeared to fly in the face of reason. In other words, the modern concepts of equality of opportunity, equality before the law, were totally alien ideas in the sixteenth century in both Spain and America.

In colonial Mexico, racial distinctions were added to traditional class distinctions. Separate laws governed each racial group. Indians, for example, had to pay an annual tribute or head tax; others did not. They were also immune from the Inquisition. Separate laws governed blacks, mulattos, and *mestizos*. Even within the dominant white population there were immunities and exceptions. The Catholic clergy was immune from secular courts. Professions, guilds, and even universities handled their own affairs outside the jurisdiction of royal courts. In the eighteenth century, the military also received immunity from civilian courts.

Throughout the colonial period, the majority of the population consisted of Indians, even though their numbers declined radically until the eighteenth century. The majority continued to live in their own villages, where they engaged in subsistence farming. Others worked on *haciendas* or in mines. If they were fortunate enough to be under the tutelage of an enlightened official or clergyman, they could take advantage of a legal system that in theory was designed to protect them from the worst abuses. Indeed, some Indians were quite successful in winning lawsuits against Spaniards; the authorities at their best seemed to conclude that if a Spaniard had mistreated an Indian so badly that he took the case to court, he probably deserved to win. Other Indians saw urban life as an escape from the tedium of the countryside, and sought work as day laborers or servants in the cities. Nevertheless, Spaniards and *mestizos* alike looked upon Indians as lazy and uncivilized, prone to alcohol, and backward.

The white population, which dominated every aspect of colonial life, remained a minority. Many families acquired enormous wealth, and lived lives of ostentatious luxury unknown in colonial English America. High society imitated Europe, importing fine art, books, and furniture from Spain at enormous expense; status was associated with possessing imported goods from Europe as opposed to less favored domestic products. Such habits endure today, as wealthy Mexicans covet foreign products, shop abroad when possible, and frequently vacation in the United States or Europe.

Not all whites were wealthy, of course. Many struggled to maintain modest standards of living, working as foremen on *haciendas*, as village priests, or as professionals. In addition to distinctions based on class, tensions between whites born in Spain (*peninsulares*), who dominated high positions in the government and in the Church, and those born in America (*criollos*) further divided the European elite.

The original Spanish design for New Spain envisioned two cultures existing side by side. Such was not to be. Within a few generations the formal distinctions between races began to break down—not as a result of any conscious decision, but because biology made them impossible to maintain.

Since few European women accompanied the first generation of Spaniards, Indian women filled the vacuum. Some were raped or forced to become mistresses to the conquerors; others voluntarily chose to live with Spanish men, probably often for security. Even after several generations, the Spanish female population remained disproportionately low, despite complaints from the Church and laws requiring men to send for wives left behind in Spain. Moreover, it was not uncommon for married men to keep mistresses on the side.

Thus originated the *mestizo*, a mixture of Indian and European, racially descended from both races, socially a member of neither. The children of *mestizos* intermarried, and the small number of slaves imported from Africa similarly mixed with Indian, *mestizo*, and Spaniard. Despite the best effort of Spanish legal minds to create new formal categories for *mestizos* and mulattos, formal distinctions of race were gradually replaced by broader categories based on lifestyle, language, and appearance. Since there were never enough whites to fill all the jobs legally reserved for them (artisans and professionals, for example), *mestizos* assumed positions of increasing importance in the economy.

As a result, by the end of the colonial period, biology and economic necessity had eliminated race as a determinant of social class—that is, for all but the very rich, who clung to their white origins, and the very poor, those Indians who struggled to survive in their native villages.

INDEPENDENCE AND REFORM

The nineteenth century in Mexico was a period of violence and anarchy, military dictatorship and civil war, ambitious ideals and foreign occupation. Not until the last quarter of the century did Mexico begin to share in the benefits of the industrial revolution that so radically changed society in the United States and Europe. Even then, the fruits of modern capitalism and industrialization were so inequitably distributed that the twentieth century opened not with the unbridled optimism that characterized the United States, but with the first social revolution of the century.

What caused these two former colonies to experience such different histories after achieving independence? Among the many explanations historians have offered, two stand out: First, the enormous gaps between rich and poor, and between European and Indian, left Mexico less than a single cohesive nation. Social disparity was compounded by a forbidding geography that made communication difficult. To make matters worse, many in the privileged classes—landowners, clergy, military—were more interested in preserving privileges than in forging a nation. And second, there was in Mexico no consensus regarding the most basic questions a society must address, such as equality before the law, the nature of private property, the role of the Church, and the basis of legitimacy in government.

Independence

The struggle for independence from Spain demonstrated divisions that divided Mexicans from each other as much as from their mother country. It began as a social revolution led by heroic priests, Miguel Hidalgo and José María Morelos, and ended with a conservative coup designed to frustrate the dreams of those who had begun the fight ten years earlier.

New Ideas

Toward the end of the eighteenth century, a minority of Mexicans—white and *mestizo*, middle and upper class—began to question many of the premises on which traditional society was based. Influenced by the European Enlightenment and American independence, they advocated freedom of speech, a representative government, and restrictions on the power of the Catholic Church. Some began to think of independence from Spain as the only way to reform society.

These liberal reformers were also devoted to economic development. They criticized the paternalism of the *hacienda* and the autonomy of many indigenous villages, not because they kept the Indian in a state of poverty, but because they were inefficient. Education, dominated by the Catholic Church, still focused on theology and philosophy when what Mexico needed were practical skills, engineers, and economists. Spain, they argued, was a nation in decline; its restrictive traditions were a stark contrast to the dynamic market economies of England and its colonies.

Strains of Mexican liberalism began to define the root of the country's problems as "Mexico-ness," itself. Progress depended on rejecting the antiquated values inherited from Spain—as well as those of the Indian—and replacing them with the progressive values of the Anglo-Saxon world. Mexico must become something other than itself, liberals emphasized, in order to become part of the modern world.

The Hidalgo Revolt

Shortly before dawn on the morning of September 15, 1810, in the sleepy village of Dolores (today Dolores Hidalgo) in the Bajío, the parish priest Miguel Hidalgo rang the bell of the small church there to call his Indian parishioners together in the central square. In the most famous speech of Mexican history, Hidalgo called on his parishioners to free themselves from three centuries of exploitation by the Spaniards, and demand their rights as patriots. He concluded, "Long live Our Lady of Guadalupe! Long live Mexico! Death to bad government! Death to the *gachupines!*" (*Gachupines* was the derogatory term for whites born in Spain.)

Hidalgo was already known to the Spanish authorities as a troublemaker. Called before the Inquisition earlier for his heretical views on papal infallibility and the Virgin birth, he had become by 1810 more interested in the worldly condition of his poverty-stricken charges than in their eternal salvation. With Ignacio Allende, an army officer, and others, he had organized a so-called literary club whose real goal was to plot independence from Spain. Word of their plans reached the authorities; fearing imminent arrest, Hidalgo decided to initiate the uprising on his own. Thus, the struggle for independence was underway.

The band of poorly armed peasants, joined by a squad of militia, went first to neighboring San Miguel le Grand (today San Miguel Allende), which they easily conquered. The small army, inspired by their hatred of three hundred years of oppression, quickly became a mob out of control; angry Indians roamed the

75

Miguel Hidalgo.

streets, killing every European they encountered. A few days later, the movement occupied and terrorized Celaya. Next, they marched on wealthy Guanajuato, where the authorities planned a defense in a large stone granary there, the *alhóndiga*. After several fruitless efforts, Hidalgo's forces overcame the defenders, massacred soldiers and civilians alike, and pillaged the city. The suppressed resentment of centuries had exploded in a few short weeks of violence.

By mid-October Hidalgo's forces numbered over eighty thousand. Zacatecas, Valladolid (today Morelia), and San Luis Potosí fell to the rebels. On October 30, the first full-scale battle took place at Monte de las Cruces, midway between Toluca and Mexico City, between a large deployment of the Spanish army and the forces of independence. Hidalgo's numbers overcame well-trained troops, despite high casualties. Mexico City was within reach and vulnerable; independence seemed at hand.

But Hidalgo hesitated. Short of supplies, either fearing widespread desertion now that his troops had experienced the horror of battle, or perhaps the destruction his forces would wreak on the capital, Hidalgo decided to withdraw to the west. Despite additional engagements near Guadalajara, Hidalgo was in retreat. He finally was captured the following March at Monclova in Coahuila, tried by the Inquisition, and then executed. His head was returned to Guanajuato where is was displayed with the heads of other revolutionary leaders on the four corners of the granary there.

Despite its short duration, the Hidalgo crusade was a turning point in Mexican history. It associated independence with radical social reform. No longer could the social elites convince themselves that the Indian population was content in its position of subservience and poverty. For the poor, Hidalgo represented the possibility of an alternative society, a dream that would resurface

Aerial view of Guanajuato, mining city during the colonial period. Notice how the churches dominate the skyline. City is constructed in a narrow valley.

in the future. In the twentieth century, the name of Miguel Hidalgo has become associated with the nation itself: his call for independence is repeated every September 15 by the president of the Republic. Statues of the ill-fated priest are everywhere, and every city and town has dedicated one of its main streets to his memory.

José María Morelos

After the death of Hidalgo, another priest, José María Morelos, a *mestizo*, assumed control of the independence movement. Less impulsive than his predecessor, Morelos organized a smaller, better-disciplined army that waged guerrilla warfare until his capture in 1815. At the movement's height, Morelos controlled most of Mexico south of the capital.

Morelos also recognized the need to articulate the objectives of the movement. At the Congress of Chilpancingo (in the state of Guerrero), delegates outlined the principles that defined liberalism for a half-century: constitutional government, universal male suffrage, civil liberties, and an absence of government participation in the economy. He compromised only on the issue of religion: Catholicism would remain Mexico's official religion.

Meanwhile, the Spanish authorities organized a counterattack. They gradually reconquered much of the land seized by the independence movement, even as the rebels themselves could not agree on a leader after the capture of Morelos. By the end of the decade, the forces fighting for independence were little more than isolated bands, as much bandits as a force of patriots. The idealistic principles of Chilpancingo were little more than distant dreams.

José María Morelos.

Iturbide and Independence

By 1820, Mexico was tired of war and violence. American-born whites faced an additional dilemma: they craved independence from Spain, with many envisioning a more liberal society, but feared the social upheaval and redistribution of wealth that were part of the independence agenda. Could not independence be achieved without threatening the existing social fabric?

Agustín de Iturbide, an infantry officer born in Spain, decided to exploit this frustration. He arranged a meeting with the principal guerrilla leader, Vicente Guerrero, to discuss a compromise position. Out of their negotiations came the Plan of Iguala, a simple three-point program designed to have wide appeal: Mexico would be independent, and governed by a constitutional monarchy in which the Church would maintain its traditional privileges. All whites would be equal under the law. The document even praised Spain's colonizing enterprise.

To the liberals who had fought so long for independence, something was better than nothing; reform could come later. To conservatives and the white elite, the Plan of Iguala promised an unthreatening transition to independence that preserved the status quo.

For the moment, at least, Mexico was virtually unanimous in its support for the plan. Spain realized the situation was hopeless, and offered only token resistance. Thus, after 302 years of colonial rule, Mexico became independent in September 1821.

In reality, independence had been stolen by the conservatives—and had solved little. Mexico was still bitterly divided over the form its government and society would take. The elite that had ruled Mexico for three centuries were still in control, only the

Agustín de Iturbide.

veneer of Spanish bureaucracy was gone. It is indicative of the anticlimactic character of the final achievement of independence that today there is no celebration of the event; September 15, the date of Hidalgo's cry for independence, remains today as Mexico's Independence Day.

Anarchy and Despotism

The Mexico that achieved independence in 1821 was huge, extending from Guatemala in the south to present-day Oregon in the north. It was also a country in shambles. The wars themselves had wreaked havoc on the economy. There was no bureaucracy in place, not even an agreement on the form the new government should take. The issues raised by liberal reformers and Hidalgo's radicals remained unresolved.

The first five decades of Mexican independence were a time of political anarchy and economic stagnation. Local and regional strongmen, known as *caudillos*—men on horseback who, with their followers, saw themselves as national saviors—contended for power in the name of competing ideologies. A series of dictatorships, interrupted by frequent military coups, disguised a reality in which no one was really governing the country. Powerful families and the Church maintained their hold over the population regardless of who was nominally in charge far off in Mexico City. The economy drifted since the political chaos discouraged new investment. Liberal and conservative intellectuals debated abstract principles, both favoring weak government—conservatives in the name of *fueros*, liberals in the name of Jeffersonian democracy. Neither recognized that the lack of effective government was at the heart of Mexico's problems.

The most significant events during this period were two wars with the United States, wars that cost Mexico half of its national territory. Yet, what was left of Mexico in 1855 was little different from the Mexico of 1821. Indeed, even today one is hard-pressed to find a single structure of significance built during this tragic period.

Emperor Agustín I

Once independence had been accomplished, Iturbide realized the new nation needed a symbol behind which it could unite. He also mistook the all-but-unanimous support for independence for support of himself.

In May 1822, Iturbide, in response to carefully planned spontaneous demonstrations by soldiers and civilians in the capital, named himself Emperor of Mexico. During the next few months a puppet congress debated the fine points of nobility, titles, national holidays (such as the birthdays of Iturbide's children), and whether mottoes glorifying the new emperor should be in Spanish or Latin.

Few Mexicans other than die-hard conservatives wanted any part of a new imperial order. There were more important problems to address. The government was bankrupt, and bandits were terrorizing much of the countryside. Iturbide was irrelevant.

Only a few months after his coronation, Iturbide found himself facing armed revolt by frustrated military garrisons and principled liberals. In February 1823, he abdicated his throne and retreated to Europe to live in exile. Several years later, still fancying himself the savior of Mexico amidst the chaos that followed his brief reign, he returned. This time he was unceremoniously executed.

Santa Anna

The military leader of the liberal coup that had ousted Emperor Agustín I was Antonio López de Santa Anna, the man who dominated Mexican politics for the first half of the nineteenth century. Born in Vera Cruz, Santa Anna had entered the Spanish army as a teenager, and had participated in skirmishes against the Hidalgo revolt. In 1821 he supported Iturbide's program for independence, and then, two years later, came to the aid of the liberals who overthrew him. Thus, early in his career, he established the role he would play for a quarter century: national savior, above the law and above politics, who would arbitrarily and single-handedly ride to the rescue of his country when he determined that his country needed him.

Following the ouster of Iturbide, Mexicans held their first con-stitutional convention in 1824, where liberals and conservatives debated the abstract issue of federalism vs. centralism. Liberals won the presidency in Mexico's first national election in 1824, and conservatives won four years later. Neither side, however, was willing to concede to the other; both sides preferred to resort to military coups rather than tolerate their opponents in power. Hence Santa Anna, Mexico's foremost general, became the ultimate power broker. He suppressed a conservative revolt in 1827, but lent his support to a liberal revolt a year later, and ultimately forged a compromise wherein he named a liberal president and a conserva-tive vice-president. Meanwhile, he further enhanced his reputa-tion by defeating an ill-fated Spanish attempt to regain its lost colony. Santa Anna was now not only a liberal hero, but the most prominent name in the country. Any office was his for the asking. Still, he seemed unsure of what he wanted. He loved playing the

Antonio López de Santa Anna.

national savior, leading his men on his white charger to defeat the enemies of the fatherland. He loved the action, and reveled in the glory that followed. Yet, he himself possessed neither a political agenda nor a vision for Mexico, preferring to vanquish new enemies rather than deal with the massive problems his nation faced.

In 1833, after once again overthrowing a conservative president, Santa Anna decided to run for president rather than sit on the sidelines. His victory was overwhelming. A year later, however, tiring of the day-to-day tasks of government, he resigned, delegating power to his liberal vice-president, Valentín Gómez Farías. Gómez Farías, believing himself invulnerable with Santa Anna behind him, enforced his liberal agenda, especially his strident anticlericalism, with a vengeance. Conservatives now approached Santa Anna, who had withdrawn to his luxurious hacienda near Vera Cruz, to come to the salvation of his fatherland by throwing out the godless Gómez Farías. Santa Anna obliged; by early 1836 he was back in the president's chair, this time as a conservative.

Fortunately for Santa Anna, events did not give him time to become bored. Far off on Mexico's northern frontier, Texas declared its independence. Opportunity and destiny called! Texas became Santa Anna's first major defeat. (Texas and the United States-Mexican War are discussed in the next section.)

Two years later, Santa Anna found an opportunity to redeem his reputation in the so-called Pastry War against France. It was common in the nineteenth century for Europeans to use military force to compel weak Latin American nations to pay claims submitted against their citizens. Given the degree of civil violence, such claims were frequent. In 1838, France demanded immediate payment of all claims brought by French citizens in Mexico against the Mexican government, including those of a French baker whose shop had been stormed by a hungry mob. The French navy bombarded the port of Vera Cruz and prepared to force payment by taking control of the customshouse in that port city. Santa Anna rode to the rescue, driving the small French force back to the sea and forcing them to withdraw. In the course of battle, Santa Anna's leg was severely wounded, and it was later amputated. His image soared; he had now lost a limb for the fatherland. Four years later, remains of the leg were carried in formal procession to Mexico City where, in a magnificent ceremony attended by the full cabinet and diplomatic corps, a formal burial was staged.

The legacy of Santa Anna was devastating for Mexico. When he was ousted for the last time in 1855, Mexico may well have been worse off than when it was a colony under Spain. Power on the local level remained in the hands of landowners and the Church. On the national level, Mexico had yet to agree on a legitimate government; power rested on armed force. The economy was in one long recession. Extremes between rich and poor were, if anything, worse; nothing so vividly symbolized the tragic fate of most Indians and *mestizos* as the *cargador*, the human pack animal who carried goods through the capital. It was cheaper to use human beings to move materials than animals!

Texas and War with the United States

From the perspective of later generations, the principal tragedy of the Santa Anna years was the loss of half of Mexico's territory to the United States. The sorry state of political leadership in Mexico was no match for North America's arrogant Manifest Destiny. How different might Mexico be today if it possessed the oil of Texas, the rich grazing land of the Southwest, and the fertile agricultural valleys of California.

At the time of independence, what is now the United States' Southwest was Mexico's frontier. With the exception of what is now northern New Mexico, the territory was largely populated by Native Americans. Only a few trading posts and former mission sites—Los Angeles, Santa Fe, San Antonio—had established a Spanish presence in the region.

In 1821, Stephen Austin negotiated a concession from the new Mexican government whereby settlers from the United States would be allowed to purchase land at bargain-basement prices in Texas. From Mexico's perspective, the concession was an inexpensive way to develop the frontier. To the immigrants, the rich soil of East Texas represented an opportunity to expand the cotton-slave culture of the South. By 1835, there were 30,000 Anglo inhabitants and only 7,500 Mexicans in the region. At first, Mexico had hoped to integrate the immigrants into Mexican society. Efforts failed, however, as the Anglo settlers, despite nominal pledges of loyalty, maintained their American identity. Conflicts arose between the Anglo and Mexican inhabitants of the region. In the early 1830s, Mexico, realizing it had a growing alien population within its borders, attempted to restrict further immigration. The conservative, centrist regime that came to power in 1835 was determined to "re-Mexicanize" its northern territory by enforcing Mexico's prohibition against slavery and its requirement that the inhabitants of Texas convert to Roman Catholicism.

Texas leaders renounced the new decrees enforcing integration into Mexico, declaring that they broke the original understandings of semi-autonomy. What followed has been immortalized in countless movies. Santa Anna, never one to resist a challenge, marched north to compel obedience at all costs. Texas patriots sought refuge in the Alamo, a former Franciscan mission. Great courage was exhibited by both sides; the Texans vowed to fight to the death, and Santa Anna obliged them. The overwhelming numbers of the Mexican army finally broke through the Texan defenses; Santa Anna ordered all the Texans shot, whether they surrendered or not. Several weeks later, another Texas army surrendered to Santa Anna at Goliad. Here, too, the *caudillo* ordered the prisoners executed. Word of Santa Anna's brutality brought new recruits to the remnants of the Texas force. On April 21, the Texas army defeated Santa Anna at the Battle of San Jacinto, near present-day Houston, and compelled him to recognize Texas' independence.

Texas remained an independent republic for ten years, its independence assured once the United States and England recognized the new state. Most Texans, however, thought of themselves as Americans, and sought annexation to the United States. At first, North American officials were hesitant, some fearing war with Mexico, others reluctant to admit an additional slave state. In 1845, however, President James Polk, who had campaigned on a platform of Manifest Destiny, signed into law the annexation of Texas as the twenty-eighth state.

During the next two years, relations worsened between the United States and Mexico. The two countries disagreed on the border: Mexico claimed it was the Nueces River (near present-day Corpus Christi), and the United States claimed it was the Rio Grande. The issue was not the 150 miles that separated the two in south Texas, but what is now much of west Texas, New Mexico, and Colorado. Mexico was justifiably suspicious that the border dispute was an excuse for the United States to acquire all of California. Both nations sent troops to the disputed border; after a minor skirmish, the United States declared war on Mexico.

The sorry condition of the Mexican government and its ill-equipped armed forces were no match for the United States. American troops occupied Santa Fe and California without encountering opposition. General Zachary Taylor defeated Santa Anna's troops at Buena Vista, near Saltillo. General Winfield Scott invaded near Vera Cruz, where he blockaded and bombarded the city mercilessly, denying the pleas of foreign consuls to allow women and children to withdraw. There were over one thousand civilian casualties.

The way was now clear to Mexico City. Taylor skillfully circumvented Mexican defenses along the way, and entered Mexico City from the south. Despite courageous resistance, the Mexicans were finally forced to capitulate. Their final defense was made at Chapultepec Castle, defended by troops and cadets of the military academy. As the Americans mounted the barricades of the fortress, young cadets threw themselves over the wall, preferring to die rather than surrender to the invaders. In the imposed peace agreement that followed, Mexico ceded California and the entire Southwest to the United States.

For most Americans, the war with Mexico is a remote memory from eighth-grade history classes. For Mexicans, the war happened yesterday, and remains an enduring scar that demonstrates the need for constant vigilance against the arrogant, aggressive "Colossus to the North." Many Mexicans feel that the United States stole half of its territory. The war and the brutality that accompanied it on both sides also contributed to the stereotypes each combatant held of the other: aggressive, uncultured Americans; lazy, backward Mexicans.

La Reforma

The liberals that overthrew Santa Anna in 1855 were a new generation. Deeply patriotic, they viewed the defeat by the United States as final proof of the bankruptcy of the society inherited from Mexico's colonial past. They envisioned a modern, progressive state where the rule of law would replace the regional *caudillos* and military anarchy, and where individual political and economic freedom would replace the traditional society of fixed social orders. Mexico needed to be a nation, they believed, in which all inhabitants were citizens, sharing opportunities and the right to determine their own future. Government had the obligation to improve the lives of its citizens. But before these lofty goals could be achieved, the extra-legal power of the Church, the army, and the regional *caudillos* first had to be destroyed. The reformers, who included some of the most thoughtful intellectuals of their generation, moved quickly to change the very fabric of Mexican society, first through legislation, and then with the comprehensive constitution of 1857.

The most prominent among this generation of liberal reformers was Benito Juárez, a Zapotec Indian from a small village in Oaxaca. Overcoming all odds, he had earned a law degree, entered politics, and even had won an election as governor of his home state. His attention turned to the national scene, where, as Minister of Justice, he sought to legislate out of existence the evils of the colonial legacy.

La Reforma, as the program of liberal reconstruction became known, first attacked traditional legal privilege. All *fueros*, those privileges possessed by members of the clergy and the army that exempted them from the jurisdiction of civilian courts, were abolished; priests and soldiers were no longer outside the law. The reformers also deprived the Church of its traditional role in recording births, marriages, and deaths, and prohibited corporations such as the Church and religious orders from owning property not directly related to their religious functions. Finally, the constitution of 1857 ignored Catholicism's traditional role as an official religion, and guaranteed freedom of speech, education, and assembly for all. In a single blow, the Mexican Catholic Church lost its monopoly over religion, its immunity from government interference, and most of its wealth. It also lost its traditional role as arbiter and protector of public and private morality. The Church responded by declaring the constitution null and void.

The reformers were particularly determined to destroy the Church's economic base in order to insure their reforms could not be undone, and, at the same time, to redefine the nature of private property. Since colonial days, up to one-half of all the land in Mexico had been owned by corporations—religious orders, charitable institutions, municipal authorities, and those Indian villages that had never been incorporated into *haciendas*. Under the laws of the reformers, corporations were allowed to retain only that real estate used directly in daily operations; what they traditionally had held as endowment, or source of income, was to be sold at public auction. Within six months, the Catholic Church saw some $20 million of its property transfer to private hands.

The administration of the new laws radically changed the Mexican economic landscape. The Church lost for all time the huge landholdings that traditionally had given it its economic clout. *La Reforma*, however, was not a radical program designed to redistribute the nation's wealth. Since confiscated land was sold, only those with assets or sources of credit were able to take advantage of the unrealistically low prices. Few landless peasants had the resources to purchase land, and those that did were often intimidated by local clergy. As a result, the principal beneficiaries of the land redistribution were existing landowners who increased their holdings; reform favored the entrepreneur, not the poor.

The property laws of *La Reforma* also destroyed the *ejido*, the land traditionally held in common by Indian villages since before the time of the conquest. The liberal reformers clearly hoped to transform the traditionally communal Indian culture into a society of independent farmers. Private land ownership, they hoped, would open the door to individual initiative. In other words, these liberal reformers, dedicated to the ideal of individual political and economic freedom, hoped to convert an Indian society structured around communal ownership of village land into a nation of entrepreneurs. Private property and economic opportunity would allow the Indians to become active, productive citizens in the Mexico of the future.

Reformers have debated the relative merits of private vs. communal ownership in Mexico since then. Should the nation honor the cultural traditions of its poorest inhabitants, or force their entry into a modern market economy? Later Mexican history proved that both solutions exacted a terrible price. In any event, the short-term effect of the reform was disastrous for the Indian communities. Few Indians possessed the resources to purchase the land their ancestors had farmed for generations. As a result, the principal impact of the abolition of the *ejido* was to provide owners of neighboring estates with the opportunity to increase their holdings at the expense of nearby Indian villages. (To be sure, few *ejidos* were sold during the initial years of *La Reforma*. But the laws of the period became the legal and moral justification of widespread confiscation of Indian lands during the Díaz dictatorship.)

Civil War and Intervention

Opposition to liberal reform came not from isolated Indian villages, but from the Catholic Church. Bishops condemned the reforms and threatened with excommunication anyone who purchased confiscated Church land—ultimately even those who pledged an oath of loyalty to the nation's elected government. Even Pope Pius IX condemned the government and its laws. Civil War was inevitable with the Catholic Church the symbol of all that was good as well as bad in Mexican society.

The Three-Years War, or War of the Reform, that engulfed Mexico between 1858 and 1861 was one of the most destructive in its history. Both sides agreed the outcome would determine the future of Mexico. On one side were the forces of religion and tradition, convinced that they were protecting civilization against anarchy. Opposing them were the forces of individual freedom and democracy, equally convinced that only through comprehensive reform could Mexico become a modern nation. Noncombatants were forced to choose sides or risk death. Even those who offered medical assistance or spiritual solace to the enemy were executed as traitors. Indian villages supported both factions, some siding with the liberals because they promised a better life, others siding with the conservatives because the liberals had confiscated village lands.

After three years and tens of thousands of casualties, the liberals were finally victorious, and Benito Juárez assumed the presidency. Mexico desperately needed a time of peace to recover from the rav-

Benito Juárez.

ages of the fighting. But such was not to be. Although they had been defeated on the battlefield, the most recalcitrant among the conservatives were not yet willing to concede the country to a liberal regime. In a last desperate ploy, they looked to Europe for help.

By this time, European nations had become increasingly frustrated with Mexico's refusal to pay legitimate debts owed to their citizens. In 1861, Juárez, facing an empty treasury, announced a moratorium on all foreign debt payments. England, Spain, and France decided to seize the customshouse in Vera Cruz, collect tariffs on goods entering the country, and use the funds to pay off the debts. The combined forces of the three countries occupied Vera Cruz in December 1861.

France had more ambitious plans, however. Napoleon III dreamed of emulating the conquests of his uncle, Napoleon Bonaparte, by creating a vast empire of "Latin" peoples under the hegemony of France. (The term "Latin America" dates from this time.) Mexico presented the ideal opportunity to extend French influence into the New World. The timing was perfect; the United States, opposed to any European intervention in the Western Hemisphere, was involved in its own Civil War. Mexican conservatives in Paris assured the French emperor that his troops would be welcomed by all God-fearing Mexicans.

Once the British and Spanish became aware of France's larger intentions, they quickly withdrew. Napoleon III reinforced his own troops, and ordered them to march toward the capital, expecting little resistance. Near Puebla, however, Mexican forces successfully overwhelmed the French and forced them to withdraw. A young cavalry officer, Porfirio Díaz, who would dominate Mexican history for the last third of the century, played a decisive role in the Mexican victory.

The site of the Mexican victory, one of the few Mexico has ever enjoyed against a foreign invader, is today a national monument. The Mexican fortifications have been restored, and are easily accessible from Puebla. Every year on May 5 (cinco de mayo), the victory is celebrated as a major national holiday.

The victory was only temporary, however. With the help of reinforcements, the French again laid siege to the city of Puebla, and eventually, after starving the residents, forced its surrender. Juárez, realizing the capital was indefensible, withdrew from Mexico City in order to regroup and harass the invaders in the countryside. Once again, it seemed the conservatives controlled the capital.

Emperor Maximilian

Napoleon III had not sent thousands of his best troops across the Atlantic simply to take sides in Mexico's interminable factionalism. His ambitions were far more grandiose: he wanted to install a European monarch on a Mexican throne. He and his conservative Mexican advisers decided upon the Hapsburg prince Maximilian as the perfect ruler for Mexico.

Maximilian was an enigmatic, even tragic, figure, raised in the best traditions of the antiquated concept of *noblesse oblige*. He wanted to be loved by his subjects (conservatives assured him this would be the case), and to provide Mexico with enlightened rule. He and his young bride, Carlota, arrived in Vera Cruz in 1864.

His reception was not what he expected. Local residents either avoided the welcoming ceremony or turned their backs. Only when Maximilian and Carlota reached Mexico City did they receive the welcome they had hoped for, organized by the conservatives and

Maximilian.

the Catholic hierarchy. The monarchs established themselves in Chapultepec Castle (site of the final resistance to the North American invaders only fifteen years before) and attempted to draw an uneasy balance between immersing themselves in the local culture and recreating the lifestyle of European monarchs. Maximilian refurbished the castle and began construction of what is today the Paseo de la Reforma, a broad boulevard originally designed to facilitate his journey from the castle to the seat of government in the National Palace.

Maximilian sincerely tried to be the enlightened ruler. He welcomed Indian petitioners into the castle, promoted modernization of the capital, and gave generously from his own resources to the poor. He antagonized conservatives by refusing to restore the Church property confiscated by the liberals.

Despite his good intentions, however, Maximilian never really governed Mexico. Most of the countryside remained in the hands of the liberals fighting under Benito Juárez. Maximilian deceived himself into believing that the Mexican people really loved him; only a few bandits stood between him and his subjects. He pleaded to Napoleon III for more troops.

Napoleon III, meanwhile, had become disillusioned with his Mexican adventure. In the United States, the Civil War now over, Washington was making serious threats about using its victorious army to drive the French from the continent. In Europe, Bismarck and Prussia were a more serious threat to France than Mexican bandits. Napoleon III decided to withdraw his forces from Mexico. Carlota, who had returned to Paris to make a last plea on behalf of her husband, wisely recognized that the regime would not survive without the presence of the French army. Her husband, still convinced that his duty lay in Mexico, refused to withdraw. He was

The Paseo de la Reforma.

captured by liberal forces in 1866 and executed by firing squad near Querétaro.

The Liberal Republic

The execution of Maximilian marked the final demise of the conservative cause and the beginning of modern Mexico. Benito Juárez received a triumphant reception in the capital, riding in a plain black coach that stood in sharp contrast to the ostentation of Maximilian's luxurious coach.

Juárez called for elections in 1867, and was overwhelmingly elected to the presidency. He ran again for the presidency four years later, this time against two liberal opponents including Porfirio Díaz, the hero of the battle of Puebla. While the results were still being debated, Juárez suddenly succumbed to a heart attack. (It was widely believed at the time that he had been poisoned.) In 1876, Porfirio Díaz overthrew by force Juárez's successor, Sebastián Lerdo de Tejada, demonstrating that Mexico had yet to overcome a tradition whereby force still rode roughshod over constitutional succession.

The years of the republic between Maximilian and Porfirio Díaz were good ones for Mexico, despite the destruction wrought by ten years of internecine warfare. Juárez was determined to use his popularity to transform Mexico into a modern nation, with special attention given to economic development, education, and peace in the countryside.

The key to economic development was the introduction of modern technology. Under Juárez, Mexico constructed its first railroad from Mexico City to Vera Cruz, and the grand Buenaventura railroad station in the capital, still in use today. Roads were improved

Dramatic railroad photos, late 19ᵗʰ century.

throughout the countryside, and gaslights introduced in the capital. The *Rurales*, a rural police force, was established to stamp out banditry and bring law and order to the countryside.

Juárez's special interest was education, the institution that had enabled him to escape from poverty. Public education was declared a universal right, and although the number of schools could never meet popular needs, the number of students attending school almost doubled between 1857 and 1876.

The Porfiriato

When Porfirio Díaz came to power in 1876, Mexico was less advanced in comparison with the rest of the world than it had been as a Spanish colony at the start of the century. The majority of the population struggled to subsist on small plots of land; only a small minority of the population enjoyed the material comforts that had become commonplace in Europe and North America. Mexico had yet to enjoy the fruits of the industrial and technological revolutions of the nineteenth century. Military anarchy, divisive civil wars, and foreign intervention had effectively stalled economic and political development.

Porfirio Díaz ruled Mexico with an iron fist, both directly and indirectly, from 1876 to 1910, a period known as the *Porfiriato*. Díaz was determined to force Mexico to join the modern world at any cost. He surrounded himself with a new breed of intellectuals, dubbed científicos, whose analysis of Mexico's backwardness guided government policy. Such imported ideologies as Positivism and Social Darwinism, completely alien to the Mexican experience, provided a philosophical underpinning for the regime.

Díaz and his advisers were convinced that the road to economic

Right: *Porfirio Díaz.*
Below: *Indigenous mother and child, c. 1910.*

development lay in the kind of unbridled capitalism that appeared to have been such a success in the United States and England. Government had to create a political climate that would be attractive to foreign capitalists whose investments, in turn, would become the engine for developing a dynamic Mexican economy. Mexicans who collaborated with the development enterprise through hard work and careful investments would share in the profits. Those who lacked the will or the resources to join this brave new world of Anglo-Saxon capitalism, or rejected its values, would be left behind. The vast majority of Mexicans who had nothing to contribute but their labor would be transformed into a docile, obedient working class that would attract investment.

Since progress was associated with emulating Anglo-Saxon habits and values, the Díaz regime endeavored to present to the world the image of a modern European nation, even to the point of suppressing popular culture. Traditional pastimes, from bullfights to folk dances, were prohibited in areas where they might be seen by foreigners. Beggars were driven from streets frequented by visitors. At times of official functions, anyone wearing traditional garb was unceremoniously removed, lest Mexico's new modern image be tarnished. Instead, artists from abroad were welcomed into Mexico, where they performed in modern theaters designed to look European, not Mexican. Wealthy families imitated the customs of the European elite, built homes designed by foreign architects, and sent their children to boarding schools abroad. Baseball was introduced to encourage the middle classes to relax as Americans did.

In order to attract foreign investment, the Díaz regime was determined to impose law and order on Mexico, whatever the cost. It tolerated little criticism; unfriendly newspapers were shut down by gangs of thugs, and their editors arrested. In the countryside, the *Rurales* became the private army of Díaz and the capitalists. They ruthlessly suppressed with brutal efficiency the smallest sign of discontent: most prisoners were "shot while trying to escape," a euphemism for avoiding the nuisance of trial and imprisonment. (The *Rurales* were also an important balance against the army, effectively discouraging any thoughts of a military coup.) Strikes were strictly prohibited; investors were assured they would not have to deal with any labor problems.

Law and order was not only an end in itself, but the necessary prerequisite to attracting foreign investment for economic development. Aided by conservative fiscal policies that appealed to foreign bankers, the regime experienced spectacular success in attracting foreign capital. Foreigners eagerly bid for concessions offered to re-open mines, build railroads and utility networks, and drill for oil. The government aided Mexican and foreign investors alike in acquiring land by confiscating lands traditionally owned by indigenous villages and small landholders alike, usually on the pretext of faulty deeds. By the end of the *Porfiriato*, wealth and land ownership were far more concentrated than ever before.

One-time conservatives found they could prosper under this new brand of liberalism. The Church, though still deprived of its previous wealth, recovered its traditional influence. Landowners enjoyed new economic opportunities. A fledgling middle class welcomed new opportunities for middle-management positions in government and in the new industrial concerns.

In any event, the regime achieved its economic objectives beyond its wildest dreams. Within a single generation, Mexico became a major exporter of minerals—especially silver and copper—and, for a time, was a principal source of the world's oil. Foreign trade grew five-fold. Manufacturing complemented the growth in

The Rurales.

Peasants at work in a factory, under the watchful eye of the Rurales.

Rare textile strike during the Díaz years.

Renaissance-style post office, built under Díaz, still in use today.

the extraction of raw materials with the establishment of industrial concerns that produced steel, textiles, building materials, leather goods, and processed food.

By 1910, Mexico was well on the way to becoming a modern nation respected on the world scene. Mexico enjoyed a dynamic economy whose potential for future growth seemed unlimited. Modernization had occurred at a tremendous price, however; it is not an exaggeration to assert that Mexico had become a modern nation at the expense of the Mexican people. Nowhere was the contrast between the elite and the poor more dramatic than on the rural *hacienda*.

During the *Porfiriato*, landowners had increased their holdings at the expense of the peasantry. In the most productive areas of the country, the *hacienda* completely dominated the land; small or communal holdings were but a past memory. Peasants working on the *hacienda* were completely at the mercy of the landowner. They were forced to purchase necessities at the *hacienda* store for inflated prices, usually on credit. Mysterious fees were added to accounts, so that there was no way a peasant could ever hope to get out of debt. Laws enforced by the hated *Rurales* prohibited them from leaving the *hacienda* until all debts were paid. As a result, the peasants were virtual slaves, completely at the mercy of the landowners and their foremen, beyond any protection of the law. Corporal punishment and sexual violation of young women were not uncommon. The influence of the *hacienda* extended to nearby villages through alliances among landowners and local political bosses. Thus, in rural Mexico there was ruthlessly enforced order, but little law.

The Revolution

As Mexico prepared to celebrate the centenary of its independence in 1910, it was a vastly different country from what it had been only thirty years before. The countryside was at peace. Modern railroads crisscrossed the country, carrying the oil and mineral exports that made it a major source of raw materials to the world. Nascent industry seemed to promise ever greater prosperity. Stability had won for Mexico a respected place in the world community.

Yet, beneath the surface all was not well. Workers and miners, paid barely enough to survive, were brutally suppressed when they attempted to organize. In the countryside, the vast majority of the population lived no better than the animals that belonged to their landowner, to whom they were in perpetual debt. Indeed, it seemed that Mexican prosperity had been earned at the expense of the majority of the Mexican people, most of whom were probably worse off than they had been one hundred years before.

Even many among the young generation of the middle and upper classes—the very classes that had prospered during the Díaz years—were discontent. Some sought the liberal ideas of free speech and free elections that had been sacrificed for economic growth. Others resented thinking of themselves as outsiders in their own country, and longed for a Mexican identity and culture that had roots in Mexico's own rich heritage.

Violent Revolution, 1910-1920

The Mexican Revolution of 1910, the first major social revolution of the twentieth century, lasted ten long years. During the course

Palace of Fine Arts, constructed for the centenary of independence by the Díaz regime. After a century of slowly sinking into the lake bed on which Mexico City is built, one today walks down *to enter the theater.*

Rural village in the 1920s.

of the fighting, between one and two million people were killed, one out of every eight Mexicans. Millions more were uprooted from their homes. The economy was left in ruins. Not a single revolutionary leader died a natural death. The national institutions that had been carefully crafted by nineteenth-century liberals were no more. Once again, Mexico faced the awesome task of creating a nation out of the ruins of anarchy and destruction.

Francisco Madero

The Revolution began in the north, Mexico's frontier. The states of Sonora and Chihuahua, adjacent to the United States, had a long history of rugged individualism and resistance to the central government in far-off Mexico City. Its mestizo population lacked the tradition of self-contained Indian villages and Spanish colonial paternalism.

Francisco Madero was an idealistic landowner devoted to the liberal traditions of Benito Juárez. Díaz, he believed, had violated the tradition of constitutional government by suppressing civil liberties and becoming, in effect, dictator for life. In the months prior to the centennial celebration, Madero had traveled throughout Mexico building a modest liberal opposition with the theme, "Effective suffrage, no re-election!" Eventually forced to flee to the United States, Madero called for a national uprising to force a return to constitutional government.

Madero had touched a nerve. On the appointed day, November 5, uprisings occurred throughout Mexico, especially in the north. Bands of peasants, shopkeepers, and workers came together spontaneously, and attacked government outposts. In the course of the fighting, leaders emerged that formed the nucleus of the revolution-

Francisco Madero.

ary leadership for years to come. The military, with an old and self-satisfied officer corps, seemed unable to meet the challenge. During the next few months, city after city fell to rebel bands. Finally, in May, Díaz submitted his resignation to congress and boarded a ship for Europe. The revolutionaries were victorious.

When Madero entered Mexico City, the nation was jubilant. Madero looked forward to a new era of constitutional government rooted in democratic principles and individual rights. In the fall of 1911, he was overwhelmingly elected president. Even before he took office, however, divisions had appeared among the revolutionary leaders. The leaders who had made the Revolution possible had more radical objectives.

For Madero, the objectives of the Revolution had been primarily political. Process was all-important; reforms could only be initiated through due process, after a constitution had been written and laws crafted. For the time being, he governed through the institutions he had inherited from Díaz, and refused to disband the army.

Among the revolutionaries themselves, however, there was far less agreement. They had joined the fight against Díaz because Díaz represented everything that was wrong with Mexico, not because they agreed upon what was to be done next. For most, the Revolution had already become a cause far greater than the modest political reform envisioned by Madero. Revolution meant change at every level of society, not merely a return to constitutional government. Peasants demanded land; workers organized and demanded a larger voice in industry; social reformers demanded the expansion of educational opportunities. The principal revolutionary armies refused to lay down their arms until their more radical demands were met. Liberals felt cheated by Madero's deliberate caution.

For the moment, however, Madero faced a more pressing threat from the Right. In 1912, Felix Díaz, the former dictator's nephew, taking advantage of the discord among the revolutionaries, attempted a coup designed to restore the stability of the Díaz years. The army was divided. Madero called on Adolfo de la Huerta to suppress the rebels. The battle began in Mexico City, bringing the violence of Revolution to the capital for the first time. The worst fighting occurred around the Ciudadela, today a city library, whose stone walls still display the impact of bullets. Fighting raged for ten days; civilian casualties far exceeded those of the combatants. Finally, Huerta decided to change sides, and arrested President Madero. The United States ambassador, Henry Lane Wilson, supervised the negotiations between Huerta and Díaz, convinced that American business would profit from an end to talk of reform. Under Wilson's guidance, Huerta was named president. (Wilson, no relation to President Woodrow Wilson, acted on his own. President Wilson immediately disavowed the agreement on behalf of the United States government.) The old regime was restored. Shortly afterwards, Huerta had Madero removed from prison and shot.

The Radical Phase

Now revolutionary chieftains once again had a common enemy: the hated *Federales* of the Huerta government. Bands of armed men arose throughout Mexico. Unsure of their own objectives, and not united behind any single leader or program, they fought only to preserve and fulfill the Revolution, whatever that meant. These revolutionary armies, each under a charismatic, courageous *caudillo* who seemed to represent the Revolution at the moment,

Henry Lane Wilson.

were fundamentally popular movements. The violence itself was liberating, as peasants acted upon the grievances they had endured for centuries. Revolution became an end unto itself; indeed, it was the actual fighting that made men free. Spontaneous folk songs, *corridas*, celebrated victories against the hated establishment. (Perhaps the best known are "Valentina," "La Cucaracha," and "Adelita," a love song. Mariano Azuela's short novel, *The Underdogs*, offers a sympathetic view of the revolutionary forces.) For the first time, the Mexican people took matters into their own hands and forged their own identity.

The Revolution was a war without rules and clearly-defined sides. Atrocities were committed by *Federales* and revolutionaries alike: prisoners were most often shot, and suspected collaborators with the enemy tortured or mutilated before being executed. Civilians were at the mercy of both sides, helpless to protect their young men from being drafted, and their daughters from being violated. All combatants lived off the land, taking food from defenseless peasants, and often destroying what was left. For the soldiers, themselves, medical care was all but nonexistent; after every engagement, far more died from wounds than had been killed in the fighting. By 1920, despite a high birth rate during the years of Revolution, the population was almost 1 million less than it had been in 1910.

Women also played an important role in the fighting. Every revolutionary band had its *soldaderas*—some wives of soldiers, some camp followers, and some committed to participating in their own liberation. Many were accompanied by children. The *soldaderas* played a critical role not only by foraging for food and preparing it for their men, but also at times by joining in the battle. They not only shared the hardships of their men, but had to follow the

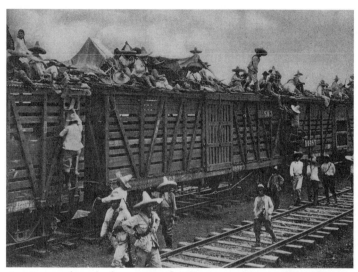

Armies move by rail, often as entire families.

Children participated in the Revolution.

mounted soldiers on foot. Yet, like the men, women found participation in the Revolution a liberating experience, and a vast improvement from the harsh life they endured on the *haciendas.*

The many small bands gradually fell under the general command of one of the principal revolutionary generals, each of whom had his own special style and vision of the Revolution. Foremost among them were Pancho Villa, Emiliano Zapata, Venustiano Carranza, and Alvaro Obregón. All marched toward Mexico City to oust the hated *Federales* and to restore the Revolution.

Pancho Villa, from Chihuahua, is perhaps the most romantic, the most charismatic, and the most controversial of the revolutionary generals. For Villa, who had lived a life of violence outside the law prior to the start of the Revolution, the purpose of the fighting was to destroy the power of the local bosses—landowners, political chieftains, bankers—once and for all. Villa instinctively recognized that the Revolution was cultural as well; civilized culture reflected a power structure that repressed the people. Thus, the orgy of violence and destruction that accompanied the arrival of the Villa forces was violence with a purpose: to destroy every vestige of ruling class power and wealth. Violence seemed the only tool available to the oppressed, for to submit to rules and laws was to submit to the status quo. Villa never developed a detailed program for the future, but it is clear that the radical upheaval he advocated was designed to destroy a culture of oppression and power.

From the south of Mexico City in the state of Morelos came Emiliano Zapata, whose forces fought under the banner of "Land and Liberty." To the predominantly Indian supporters of Zapata, talk of constitutionalism was an abstract irrelevancy. The peasants of Morelos had lost the land to expanding *haciendas* during the

Pancho Villa and his cavalry.

Early photo of Emiliano Zapata.

Classic photo of Villa and Zapata in the presidential palace.

Zapata's army on the march, including women who gathered food.

Díaz years. Now they fought to recover it. Their goal was modest: nothing more than to recover that which had been stolen, and that which was rightfully theirs. "Land and Liberty," however, would prove to be one of the Revolution's most elusive goals.

More moderate armies also converged on Mexico City from the north under the joint leadership of Venustiano Carranza and Alvaro Obregón. The *constitucionalistas*, as they were known, were heirs to Madero, open to social reform but committed primarily to democratic government. Coming from the wide open spaces of the north, Carranza and Obregón failed to appreciate the urgent need for land reform in the south.

Even President Woodrow Wilson joined the anti-Huerta coalition, uninvited, to be sure, but convinced of the North American mission to spread democracy. Using a minor skirmish between American sailors and local authorities in Tampico as an excuse, United States marines occupied the port city of Vera Cruz in 1914. Fortunately for the revolutionaries, Carranza denounced the occupation, thereby preventing Huerta from capitalizing on his role as victim of American imperialism. Ironically, the American occupation did contribute to Huerta's downfall since it deprived him of foreign arms and the revenues from the Vera Cruz customshouse. In the summer of 1914, Huerta resigned.

The ouster of Huerta removed the last obstacle to the success of the Revolution. It remained for the revolutionary generals, themselves, to determine the future Mexico would take. The struggle among the revolutionaries was one of the bloodiest of the Revolution.

Carranza, with the support of the United States, which preferred constitutional government to more radical social change, assumed the presidency after the withdrawal of Huerta. In early

Venustiano Carranza.

1914, he called a convention in Aguascalientes to determine who should assume the presidency and the direction Mexico should take. All the principal generals attended, most well-armed and not reluctant to wave their weapons at speakers with whom they disagreed. The convention clarified the deep divisions among the leaders. Should constitutional government be established, leaving social reform for an elected government? Or, should some form of land reform, the objective of both Villa and Zapata, be decreed immediately, leaving until later the writing of a constitution? When a majority sided with Villa and Zapata, the Carranza supporters withdrew; Carranza, himself, declared the convention null and void, and made himself provisional president.

Villa and Zapata promised each other mutual support, but the arrangement was short-lived. Zapata retreated to Morelos, where he initiated a far-reaching land distribution program. Villa retreated northward. For the next year, each faction claimed its own candidate to be president. Throughout Mexico, factions of each *caudillo* battled each other mercilessly. Finally, in 1915, Carranza's superior artillery defeated Villa's cavalry at the battle of Celaya, the largest pitched battle of the Revolution. Villa's strength as a viable alternative was eliminated, and Carranza prepared to rule Mexico. (Villa, furious at the United States for supporting Carranza and looking to establish his nationalist credentials, invaded the small border town of Columbus, New Mexico. In retaliation, the United States army under General Pershing chased Villa through the deserts of northern Mexico without finding him.)

Carranza served as president until 1920. Pancho Villa was allowed to retire to a *hacienda* in Chihuahua, where he was assassinated in 1923. Zapata, meanwhile, refused to lay down his arms. Carranza solved the problem of this one remaining independent

General Carranza.

revolutionary force with deception: he invited Zapata to a peace agreement, and had him shot when he entered. Carranza, himself, was assassinated in 1920 when he hesitated to surrender the presidency to his successor.

The Constitution of 1917

The most enduring legacy of the Carranza presidency was the constitution of 1917. In that year, the president called together a constitutional convention in Querétaro, minus the participation of supporters of his recent enemies. Politicians and intellectuals, not soldiers, formed the majority. Despite its unrepresentative character, the Querétaro convention approved a document that contained most of the major objectives of the revolutionaries. Although many of its articles remained promises for the future, the constitution of 1917 has endured, with minor changes, up to the present as Mexico's constitution.

The constitution reflected most effectively the objectives and principles of traditional liberals such as Francisco Madero. It limited future presidents to one term ("Effective Suffrage, No Re-Election!"). Article 3 made anticlericalism official public policy by requiring all public education to be secular as well as mandatory and free. By requiring all schools, both public and private, to follow a set curriculum defined by the state, the constitution deprived the Church of its traditional role in education. With the Revolution, Mexico moved from religious toleration to a single secular state religion. Other legislation excluded members of the clergy from participating in political life and prohibited them from wearing clerical garb in public. The state became the nominal owner of all church property, including the churches, themselves. State governments were empowered to limit the number of clergy and the number of churches. Marriage became a civil ceremony, and divorce became legal. Religious processions were banned. Priests were required to register with the local civil authorities. Foreign clergy were prohibited completely. Finally, Article 123 was an explicit bill of rights for labor that not only included the right to organize and to strike, but also guaranteed an eight-hour working day, a six-day workweek, and equal pay regardless of gender.

The most far-reaching part of the constitution, however, was Article 27, which concerned land ownership—the issue that had inspired both Zapata and Villa. Article 27 began by denying the absolute quality of private property. Henceforth, it declared, ownership was contingent on the social utility for which the land was used. Borrowing from Spanish colonial law, it declared that all subsoil wealth belonged to the state. Finally, it restricted foreign ownership of land and natural resources.

The most radical provisions of the 1917 constitution remained dormant for many years; in fact, some, such as the mandate for universal education, have yet to be fulfilled. Indeed, the constitution was more a statement of ideals and a platform for the future, than it was a constitution to be immediately imposed. Nevertheless, the document is one of the most important in Mexican history, as it has been the basis of both government initiative and public debate to the present.

Constructive Revolution, 1920-1940

In 1920, Mexico lay in ruins. Despite a high birth rate during the years of tumult, Mexico's population numbered 1 million fewer than it had a decade before. Yet, a mood of optimism prevailed. The people had spoken, and peace was finally at hand. During the next two decades, a succession of heirs to the Revolution moved to redefine the Mexican identity, implement the provisions of the 1917 constitution, and rebuild the country.

From Obregón to Calles

Alvaro Obregón, who assumed the presidency in 1920, moved quickly to start the rebuilding process. The government reopened rail lines destroyed during the fighting, and started construction of a national network of highways. With peace restored in the countryside, Mexico could again begin exporting raw materials. In order to assure foreigners, Obregón established a national bank to stabilize the currency. Prosperity slowly returned.

To be sure, the pace of reform was slow. Little land was distributed to peasants, and only those who could prove in court that their land had been stolen had it restored. Natural resources remained overwhelmingly in the hands of foreigners.

Under Plutarco Elías Calles, who succeeded to the presidency in 1924 and dominated the political system through puppets until 1934, a new class emerged. Calles, determined to prevent revolt from the new centers of power created by the Revolution, formed a political party in which generals, labor leaders, and politicians could share power. They also shared, through corruption, the fruits of their victory, building huge mansions in the hills above Chapultepec Park. Former peasants and laborers rubbed shoulders with industrialists and landowners; the Revolution had created its own route of upward mobility for those clever enough to take advantage of it. The coalition had another important effect: the army

Alváro Obregón.

Banco de Mexico.

Plutarco Elías Calles.

Mansion of the revolutionary elite, late 1920s, in Cuernavaca.

Mansion of the revolutionary elite, late 1920s, in Cuernavaca.

and organized labor were now part of the revolutionary establishment, not potential opponents to it.

The most striking reforms of these post-revolutionary years were in the areas of culture and education. Under the leadership of José Vasconcelos, the government launched a massive program to build rural schools. In an imaginative effort of government outreach, villagers joined together to construct new buildings. Typically, they included meeting rooms for adults and playgrounds as well as classrooms. Idealistic young teachers settled in remote villages, teaching the young during the day and the adults in the evening. Often public health workers established clinics in the schools, and offered rudimentary instruction on nutrition and prenatal care. For the first time, rural Mexicans received something from the central government.

The Revolution had also redefined the nature of what it meant to be Mexican. Mexicans began to take pride in their Indian heritage, and in their *mestizo* reality. Artists were encouraged to create huge murals on the walls of public buildings depicting the oppression of the past and idealizing the common man and woman. In the murals of Diego Rivera and others, Mexican history was rewritten. The Indians were the real Mexicans, the Spanish their conquerors. Despite efforts by Hidalgo and Juárez, the people remained repressed, only winning their real independence during the Revolution. In literature and music as well, Mexicans looked for their own means of expression. The traditional music and art of the people was performed and studied.

It is difficult for North Americans to appreciate the impact of this shift in national consciousness. For centuries, and especially during the *Porfiriato*, both the Indian and the reality of the *mestizo* had been defined as Mexico's defect, even its shame. Only the

Revolutionary veteran.

white world was the civilized world, capable of meaningful artistic achievement. Nonwhites could only occasionally join that world by denying their heritage and culture.

In a very real sense, Mexican nationalism was born in the 1920s. Artists consciously emulated indigenous art forms, and archaeologists and anthropologists wrote in glowing terms of past civilizations. After a century of independence, Mexicans—the majority of Mexicans—were finally at home in their own country.

The Cristero Revolt

Not everyone concurred with the new revolutionary culture. In 1926, violence broke out between the Catholic Church, that symbol of a more traditional Mexico which still held the loyalty of millions, and the Revolution in what became known as the Cristero Revolt. Tragically, it pitted the supposed beneficiaries of the Revolution, the rural peasants, against those trying hardest to assist them: rural teachers and social workers.

The Cristero Revolt began when President Plutarco Elías Calles, seeking to re-establish his radical credentials in the face of racial criticism, decided to enforce the anticlerical provisions of the constitution. He prohibited religious processions, expelled foreign priests and nuns, and closed convents and monasteries. He also ordered all clergy to register with local civil authorities. The Church's reaction was quick and unexpected: it went on strike. For the next three years, there were in Mexico no Masses, no baptisms, no confessions, and no last rites for the dying.

The strike quickly became violent. Catholic leaders organized their flocks into guerrilla bands which attacked local government officials and military outposts. Fanatical peasants assaulted helpless

Cristeros.

rural school teachers and killed them with their machetes as they cried out, "¡Viva Cristo Rey!" (Long live Christ the King!), often leaving behind banners with the letters "VCR" on the corpses. The government responded in kind, hunting down priests and suspected *Cristeros* without mercy, often executing them without a trial. (Graham Greene's *The Power and the Glory* immortalizes the story from a Catholic perspective.) In 1927, *Cristero* terrorists bombed a train, killing over one hundred passengers. A year later, a fanatical mystic killed president-elect Alvaro Obregón, a revolutionary hero.

The worst of the fighting came to an end in 1929 with an uneasy truce. The government allowed exiled clergy to return and to practice their profession, and the Church agreed to have its priests register with the government. The clergy could hold religious classes in churches, but they could not run schools. Sporadic violence continued, however, until 1940 when president-elect Manuel Avila Camacho responded to a question regarding his position on the Church by stating quietly, "I am a believer."

Lázaro Cárdenas

In 1933, Calles named Lázaro Cárdenas to succeed to the presidency. Cárdenas immediately demonstrated his would be a different kind of regime by actively campaigning throughout the countryside—his victory, of course, was already assured—listening to peasants and workers and looking closely at the conditions in which they lived. Once in office, he proceeded to implement the neglected economic goals of the Revolution and the constitution of 1917. Today, Cárdenas remains the most revered of Mexican presidents, enjoying an esteem that surpasses that of both Franklin Roosevelt and John F. Kennedy.

Lázaro Cárdenas campaigning, 1933.

Cárdenas realized that political stability was the prerequisite to the reforms he envisioned. He was also determined to bring the powerless into the political system. Hence, Cárdenas reformed the political organization he had inherited from Calles, the PMR (Party of the Mexican Revolution), into a real political party based on its constituent parts. As legitimate heirs of the Revolution, workers and peasants received a privileged role. Labor was organized into the CTM (Mexican Confederation of Workers)—a blanket organization for all organized labor. A new peasant organization was constructed to parallel the CTM. Both were structured as pyramids: local (open to all), district, state, and national councils. Each chose delegates to the next level to represent their interests. The military was the third triad in the new PMR.

During the Cárdenas years, government was clearly on the side of the lower classes. The commitment to rural education increased while support for university education remained level. Government consistently sided with labor over management, acquiring for organized labor both higher wages and generous fringe benefits. Organized labor remains today a privileged segment of the working classes. However, Lázaro Cárdenas is most remembered for two initiatives—land reform and the expropriation of the oil industry—both of which have left indelible marks on Mexico's political and economic landscape.

The Ejido

Land reform has been an integral part of every twentieth century revolution. Every successful revolution, however, has not restored land to individual peasants; instead, it has created some form of

145

state farm. Mexico under Cárdenas was the exception: land reform was designed neither to fulfill an abstract ideology, nor to promote efficiency. Rather, land reform was structured to conform with the wishes and cultural traditions of the peasants who tilled the soil.

Mexican land reform under Cárdenas was based on the traditional peasant village in which land was owned in common but tilled by individual households. The ideal, deeply rooted in pre-Columbian practice, was a self-sustaining village free to make its own collective decisions. Implicitly, land confiscated from commercial *haciendas* devoted to cash crops would likely revert to producing food products for local markets.

The regulations adopted by the Cárdenas administration were straightforward. Depending on the type of soil and topography, they prescribed a minimum per capita acreage for a peasant village, and a maximum acreage for a privately-owned landholding. Wherever there existed a village whose land was below the minimum (most villages filled this requirement) and a nearby *hacienda* that possessed more than the maximum legitimate acreage, the village had the right to petition to a special court to have land confiscated from the *hacienda* and granted to the village. If the petition was granted—under Cárdenas it usually was—the *hacienda* could determine which acreage the village would receive.

Villages that participated in the program became *ejidos*, subject to special laws. The *ejido* owned the land in common; its leadership allotted individual plots to individual households. Neither an individual household nor the *ejido* as a whole was allowed to sell or mortgage the land—restrictions designed to prevent the abuses from the past in which unscrupulous speculators had deprived whole villages of their livelihood. Special government programs provided financing for *ejidos*.

Under the Cárdenas administration, some 50 million acres, more than twice the amount redistributed under all of his predecessors combined, was given over to peasant *ejidos*. On the larger *ejidos*, public schools and clinics were also built. A tradition of total dependence on the *hacienda* owner was broken once and for all. Mexican peasants became independent from a landed elite, joined together in cooperative ventures where they became the decision-makers.

The political and social success of the *ejido* is incontrovertible; nowhere, unlike agrarian reform movements elsewhere, was there any resistance from the peasants, the intended beneficiaries of the land reform program. If the *ejido* program did not produce an escape from poverty into the middle class, it did provide a sense of dignity and control unequalled elsewhere in Latin America.

On economic grounds, the *ejido* is far more controversial. Limited acreage ultimately restricted the income potential of villages; the prohibitions against sales and mortgages repressed any entrepreneurial spirit. Critics argue that productivity per acre declined as land was converted into an *ejido*, and that productivity per acre is lower on the *ejido* than on privately-owned larger properties. Defenders of the *ejido* respond that *ejido* productivity in terms of capital investment exceeds that of every other segment of the Mexican economy.

More recently, the principal threat to the viability of the *ejido* has been population growth. Since *ejido* land is finite, an expanding population is unable to support itself on a limited amount of land. Indeed, the *ejido* has been a major source of migrants to both Mexico City and to the United States. Whatever its economic merits, the *ejido* was, until recently, an icon of post-revolutionary Mexico, beyond the realm of political debate.

Lázaro Cárdenas.

Oil

Oil became the second component of Cárdenas' revolutionary legacy, a symbol of Mexican nationalism and autonomy.

The petroleum industry had long been the scene of bitter disputes between management and labor. Although wages in the Mexican oil industry were high by Mexican standards, profits remitted to Standard Oil of New Jersey (today Exxon) were proportionately even higher.

As Mexico discovered fifty years later, the petroleum industry is complex. Oil requires enormous initial capital investment and a willingness to take risks: every well is extremely costly, and only some bear a lucrative yield. Hence, it is the profits from "sure things" that support further exploration. While this argument might be convincing to stockholders, it is less so to politicians in a particular country in which oil companies are making no new investments. From Mexico's perspective, Standard Oil and other companies were earning large profits from investments made during the *Porfiriato* without making any new investments. From Standard Oil's perspective, the oilfields of East Texas were considerably more attractive.

In 1936, oil workers went on strike, seeking higher wages and fringe benefits. Over the next few years, a series of commissions and courts, undoubtedly influenced by the Cárdenas administration, sided with the unions. When the oil companies refused to accept the decision of the Mexican supreme court, Cárdenas announced the expropriation of the oil companies' properties for violation of Mexican law. Henceforth, the Mexican oil industry would be managed by PEMEX, a subsidiary of the Mexican government.

North American historians have debated the merits of Mexico's case. From the perspective of Mexico, however, the issue was not dollars but nationalism. A joint bilateral commission agreed on a just compensation; hundreds of thousands of Mexicans contributed small amounts to finance the agreement so that Mexico's petroleum industry would be Mexico's own. It was perhaps the largest outpouring of Mexican nationalism in the nation's history.

For many decades, PEMEX worked well. Mexico neither exported nor imported on a significant scale. Modest exploitation of Mexico's oil reserves supplied the country with its energy needs at below-market prices, thereby subsidizing the industrialization to come. Petroleum workers continued to prosper as the elite of Mexico's labor force. PEMEX leased gas station locations to local businessmen, often, it was rumored, only as a result of undercover payoffs. PEMEX became part of the political reward system, providing subsidized energy to the nation's industrial enterprises, jobs to employees far in excess of what efficiency would require, and franchises to favored investors. It was an arrangement that worked, at least until 1976, when Mexico found itself sitting on one of the world's major oil reserves.

Toward the end of his presidency, Cárdenas recognized the restrictions that the world economy placed on redistribution within Mexico. Land reform declined, and labor strife decreased. Cárdenas came to believe that development, as opposed to redistribution, required the good will of the industrialized nations. Mexico, having redefined the terms, was prepared to become a respectable member of the world community.

Mexicans celebrate the nationalization of oil in Mexico City.

THE RECENT PAST

Since 1940, Mexico has been at peace. A new generation whose formative years had been devoted to politics, not warfare, came to power to consolidate the accomplishments of the Revolution. Although there have been few new initiatives designed to redistribute the nation's wealth, the government has continued to spend much of its revenue on social programs. Mexico is one of few countries that can boast of consistently spending more on education than on the military.

Until now, Mexico has remained a one-party democracy; the PRI (Party of the Institutional Revolution, the descendant of the PMR formed by Cárdenas) has won virtually every election, using whatever means necessary to assure its monopoly on power. And, for many years, the system has worked well. Mexico is the only Latin American country that has not experienced a single coup, and the only country in which the military has consistently been subordinate to civilian authority.

The "Mexican Miracle"

After 1940, Mexico turned its primary focus from redistribution to economic growth, embarking on a program that emphasized industrialization and self-sufficiency. Although early Mexican industrialization benefitted from the world-wide shortage of manufactured goods created by World War II, Mexico, like other countries in Latin America, deliberately chose to base its economic development policy on the concept of import substitution.

According to the economic doctrine of the time, infant industries in Mexico could develop only if they were protected from foreign competition. Thus, the government should promote domestic industry by erecting high tariff walls designed to keep out products imported from the United States. For forty years, Mexico successfully argued that its unique position, located adjacent to the United States, should exempt it from international trade agreements. Mexico remained one of the few nations in the West to refuse to join the GATT (General Agreement on Trade and Tariffs); when oil was discovered in the 1970s, Mexico refused to join OPEC. Furthermore, Mexico was one of the few countries in the Western world in which one could not find consumer goods made in the United States or Europe.

For three decades, this protectionist economic policy formed the basis of the "Mexican Miracle." The economy experienced significant growth year after year. A cautious fiscal policy kept both inflation and the national debt at a manageable level. An expanding middle class became eager consumers of the consumer goods produced in Mexican factories. Mexican companies manufactured automobiles, major appliances, and electronic goods. By the 1960s, the nation was virtually self-sufficient in consumer goods; close to half of Mexico's gross domestic product came from manufacturing. A decade later, Sears could boast that over 95 percent of the products on its shelves had been manufactured in Mexico.

Many of the products manufactured in Mexico carried North American brand names. Since the constitution of 1917 had prohibited foreign interests from owning more than 50 percent of any enterprise, American companies formed partnerships with local investors. Mexico was an attractive place to invest, with its stable government and growing consumer class. Indeed, American companies came to dominate those industries in which ownership was most concentrated, and advertising most aggressive. Yet, Mexico was not, strictly speaking, an economic colony of the United States: local capital and management dominated even in the subsidiaries of American firms, and Mexican conglomerates as well as small companies competed with North American multinational companies.

Government was a major partner in this program of industrialization. It actively supported economic growth with protective trade policies, huge public investment in key industries, and cheap energy. Labor could no longer count on government support for excessive wage demands. Major investments in irrigation projects focused on those areas where it would support the growth of commercial agriculture. Even the structure of the PRI was expanded to include a "popular" sector, a euphemism for business and middle class interests.

For almost thirty years, Mexico was the economic success story of Latin America. Commentators referred to the "Mexican Miracle." The nation's gross national product increased every year, doubling in the sixties. A broad array of social programs enabled those Mexicans who were part of the mainstream economy to share in the new prosperity. Foreign investment slowly returned. Modern factories arose around Mexico City, Monterrey, and other urban areas to fill the needs of the growing consumer society. The middle class expanded as an entrepreneurial spirit captured the popular imagination.

Most Mexicans seemed content to sacrifice total democracy as a reasonable price for peace and prosperity. The PRI monopolized political power, resorting to fixing elections, even force, when it was occasionally challenged. Each president chose his successor, who was guaranteed victory in national elections. Meanwhile, a new class of wealthy politicians and labor leaders arose, as it became clear that corruption, too, was part of the price of single party democracy. To be sure, minority parties were tolerated, even subsidized by the PRI, in order to maintain the appearance of democracy.

Not all Mexicans shared in the new prosperity, however; the industrial boom had sharpened the contrast between the cities and the countryside. Despite continued investments in schools and in water and sewer systems, the majority of Mexico's peasants still existed at the subsistence level. Far more threatening to future prosperity and stability was the time bomb of population explosion. By 1960, the land was no longer able to support all those who lived on it. Tens of thousands migrated from the countryside to the cities, especially to Mexico City, and to the United States in search of work. The economy, despite its rapid growth, was incapable of absorbing all of the new workers. Unemployment and underemployment became endemic. Despite its impressive record of economic growth, by 1970 Mexico suffered from one of the most inequitable distributions of income in the world.

The contrast between modern, prosperous Mexico and Third World Mexico came to a head in 1968 when modern Mexico prepared to celebrate its arrival as a modern nation by hosting the Olympic Games, the first time they had been held in a Third World country. Students organized demonstrations protesting the enormous expenditures on the Olympics while thousands were unemployed. They demanded more radical programs to serve the poor and greater democracy—in sum, a return to the principles of the Revolution. As the demonstrations increased and attracted support from the middle class, the government grew wary. Clashes between demonstrators and the police escalated. Half a million people gathered in the Zócalo, the largest anti-government rally ever in Mexican history. Finally, on the night of October 2, the government responded at a peaceful demonstration at Tlatelolco, the Plaza of the Three Cultures. Police and army troops, using machine guns and often shooting at point-blank range, fired indiscriminately into the crowd. Within a few hours, more than four hundred demonstrators were killed, and many more wounded.

The Tlatelolco massacre was a turning point in modern Mexican history. It called into question the legitimacy of the PRI, whose power ultimately depended on force, not public support. More importantly, it demonstrated that millions of Mexicans had yet to share in the profits of economic development. The economy still seemed to be booming, but the magic of the "Miracle" was no more.

From Echeverría to Salinas

Although the Olympic games proceeded on schedule, 1968 was a significant turning point for modern Mexico. The massacre at Tlatelolco made clear what had only been rumored before: the PRI governed through manipulation and fraud, even repression, when necessary; it did not represent a national consensus. In addition, the demonstrations, themselves, had focused attention on the growing number of Mexicans who were still outside the national economy, barely managing to survive, despite the impressive economic gains of the previous twenty-five years.

Furthermore, the economy was in deep trouble. Although it had contributed to the development of a middle class, perhaps one-third of the population had yet to enjoy its benefits. The disparity between rich and poor had become worse than at any time since the 1910 Revolution. Since its manufacturing sector was designed for internal consumption, Mexico had to continue to rely on agriculture and mining for its principal exports. In order to maintain its exports, capital investment in irrigation projects went primarily to large agribusinesses, not to small peasant landholdings. By the early 1970s, Mexico, for the first time in its history, was forced to import corn from abroad. Even more demeaning was the fact that the principal sources of foreign exchange were tourism and funds remitted to Mexico by laborers in the United States.

Meanwhile, Mexican industry had become self-satisfied and sluggish. Since it faced no foreign competition, it enjoyed a captive market; many Mexican products were more expensive and poorer in quality than those produced abroad. A thriving black market developed in consumer goods smuggled in from the United States. Indeed, manufacturing became a major drain on the economy: it continued to import capital goods from abroad, but could not export its finished products on the world market.

To make matters worse, widespread inefficiency, outdated technology, and a declining domestic market put many companies in financial difficulty. Faced with increased unemployment if troubled firms closed down, the government bought unprofitable companies and continued to operate them. Government investment policies, originally designed to support new industries, now served only to preserve and protect companies that otherwise could not survive.

Beginning in 1970, a succession of presidents each tried to identify and implement magic bullets that would save the Mexican economy: deficit spending, oil, and subsidized exports. None of these worked, and the living standards of the average Mexican declined. Finally, President Carlos Salinas Gortari discarded the whole set of premises on which the "Mexican Miracle" had stood—

import substitution, public-private collaboration in the economy, self-sufficiency—hoping that a return to a true market economy would accomplish what government policies had failed to do.

The Echeverría Administration

In 1970, Luis Echeverría, Minister of Justice in 1968 and held largely responsible for the Tlatelolco massacre, assumed the presidency. Whether he was truly committed to social reform, or whether he was determined to salvage his reputation after the events of 1968, will never be known. His administration, however, turned out to be the most radical—and economically the most irresponsible—of any post-World War II administration.

Echeverría and his advisers apparently believed that Mexico had one last chance to bring the disadvantaged into the national economy. He immediately made openings to the Left, inviting his principal critics to become part of his administration. The government spent vast sums of money on welfare programs, and compelled private enterprise to do the same. Recognizing that the shortage of jobs was a major obstacle to progress, the government bought large shares of companies that faced bankruptcy so that they could continue to operate rather than create additional unemployment. As a result, the government's participation in the Mexican economy was greater in the 1970s than ever before. The government also initiated huge investment programs to spur economic growth, including the resort at Cancún. Once again, it seemed, government was taking the lead in social reform.

The most enduring and constructive policies of the Echeverría administration had to do with population. Since the 1930s, Mexico's population had been growing at a terrifying rate—an ironic result of improved public health and longer life expectancy. Much urban poverty and unemployment was the result of a population that was growing faster than the economy could absorb into the work force. Yet, mainstream thinking in Mexico (and in many other Third World countries) argued that population was a strength, not a problem, and that concerns expressed by the United States and others grew out of fear or racism.

The Echeverría administration was the first to recognize publicly that the population explosion was a major obstacle to economic development. It launched a mammoth publicity campaign designed to encourage smaller families, and made contraceptives available at minimal cost. Throughout Mexico—on billboards, in comic books, in radio jingles, even as the theme in popular soap operas—the message was repeated: "The small family lives better." The campaign of propaganda worked. Within just a few years, the birth rate declined significantly. To be sure, Mexico would continue to face the effects of past births for many years; over half of the population was under the age of fifteen. But, Mexico had made an important first step, and had demonstrated to other developing nations that lower birthrates were possible.

The campaign also demonstrated a new spirit of collaboration between the government and the Catholic Church. The Echeverría administration realized from the start that the Church could sabotage its family planning campaign with aggressive opposition. Fortunately, the Catholic hierarchy became a silent partner, emphasizing in a pastoral letter the need for "responsible parenthood" and the social responsibilities all must share even while providing lip service to Papal teaching on birth control. The government, meanwhile, agreed that abortion would remain illegal in Mexico (although illegal abortions have never been hard to find).

The free-spending policies of the Echeverría administration, however well-intentioned, ultimately contributed to Mexico's current economic woes. Unlike every previous administration since 1940, Echeverría ignored any pretext of fiscal responsibility. The government operated on borrowed money with abandon, acquiring huge debts from foreign banks which were all too ready to profit from what they saw to be the continuing "Mexican Miracle." Inflation approached 20 percent, a rate unheard of in Mexico. Finally, toward the end of the Echeverría administration, the government was forced to devalue the peso by 60 percent and to accept an austerity program imposed by the World Bank.

Politics worsened the situation. Echeverría wanted to establish his leftist credentials in the world community, hoping, it was widely believed, that he would be named Secretary-General of the United Nations. In 1975, Mexico supported an Arab resolution that condemned Zionism as a form of racism. North American Jews retaliated by declaring a tourist boycott of Mexico that proved exceedingly costly in foreign exchange. During the last months of his administration, Echeverría's radical rhetoric became increasingly strident. In speeches, he even talked of forcing the rich to take in the homeless to live in spare rooms. The net effect was to further encourage the flight of private capital to Europe and the United States.

Oil: Boom and Bust

Oil gave Mexico a temporary respite from its economic woes. During the 1970s, the rising price of oil on the world market stimulated PEMEX to explore new oilfields off the coast of Tabasco and Chiapas, south of Vera Cruz. What Mexico found was beyond its wildest dreams: potential reserves, second only to Saudi Arabia. Mexico immediately became a major player in a world scene that divided the world into petroleum producers and petroleum consumers.

Although Mexico never formally joined OPEC, it agreed to sell Mexican oil at world market prices. And the world price of oil kept rising. Suddenly, Mexico seemed on the threshold of having all the foreign capital needed for economic development.

The new administration of José López Portilla, who had been finance minister in the free-spending Echeverría administration, hastened to exploit the new wealth. Foreign banks competed to extend Mexico's credit, confident that future oil revenues would assure repayment. In addition to mammoth investments in oil platforms, tankers, and refineries, Mexico increased investments in highways and welfare projects. Basic commodities were so heavily subsidized that North Americans living near the border did their weekly shopping in Mexico to take advantage of the ridiculously low prices.

Oil also gave Mexico new confidence. In a world where oil meant power, Mexico was, for the first time, free to chart its own course in foreign affairs. When the United States refused to purchase Mexican natural gas at the price Mexico wanted, Mexico simply burned it off at the wellhead. Mexico recognized the rebels in El Salvador as a legitimate political force, and provided oil at reduced prices to the Sandinista regime in Nicaragua.

During the heady years of the López Portilla administration, Mexico continued to spend far more money than it received in oil revenues. In part, this was due to the nature of the petroleum industry: petroleum requires enormous investments in wells and equipment before the revenue rolls in. (In the Middle East, much of this investment had been made decades before.) North American banks, however, were only too eager to share in the bonanza with new loans.

In 1982, as the world price of oil began to decline, Mexico came to realize fully the extent to which the economy had grown dependent on oil. A slight drop in revenue brought disaster: once again the peso began to slide and inflation soared. López Portilla's attempts to blame the banking industry for the failure—he nationalized Mexican banking in the last year of his administration—did little to restore popular confidence. The Mexican government was technically bankrupt; only last minute negotiations with North American banks, themselves vastly over-extended in loans to Mexico, forestalled total disaster. At his last State of the Union Address President López Portilla, for so long the epitome of Mexico's new self-confidence in itself, wept.

What had gone wrong? Why was Mexico the only oil-exporting country to lose on the deal? In large part, Mexico had been simply overconfident, spending far more than existing oil revenues would allow. It had based its spending policies on the mistaken belief that world petroleum prices would only go up, and that it could count on the desperation of oil importers. Corruption had also increased to new heights; there was simply too much money in circulation. PEMEX managers and labor leaders became instant millionaires, while politicians in Mexico City built huge mansions in the surrounding mountains. By the time López Portilla stepped down from the presidency in 1982, Mexican cynicism had reached new heights. But, the worst was yet to come.

The Terrible Eighties

During the decade of the 1980s, Mexico suffered the worst

economic times since the Revolution. A harsh austerity program, imposed on Mexico by foreign banks as part of the price for restructuring its foreign debt, forced the government to make enormous cutbacks in subsidies, to postpone major construction projects, and to reduce spending on social programs. Despite this, inflation continued to soar, reaching at one point an annual rate over 1,000 percent; the peso continued to drop in relation to the dollar. Unemployment and underemployment reached new heights. Even those fortunate enough to keep their jobs suffered: in the early years of the decade, real personal income among the employed segment of the population decreased by one-third.

These were conditions that likely would have led to a revolution in most other Latin American countries. Yet, in Mexico, the people somehow managed to endure. Unrest was minimal, far less than during the more prosperous times of the sixties and seventies. There was a modest increase in crimes against property; the streets of Mexico City were no longer as safe as they once were. Bank robberies became so frequent that banks hired private security guards with automatic weapons to stand guard. Symbolic of the sudden change in Mexico's fortunes was the luxurious new headquarters of PEMEX, a soaring skyscraper left half complete.

The one bright spot in the Mexican economy was the *maquiladoras*, the assembly plants that had grown up in cities bordering the United States. The concept, originally approved by both the American and Mexican governments during the 1960s, was simple: use cheap Mexican labor to assemble American parts for American products in large factories on the border. Since the parts originated in the United States, only the modest "value added" through Mexican labor was subject to duties when the finished products were shipped back across the border. *Maquiladoras* were particularly popular in the electronics industry. Both sides benefitted: American producers lowered costs, and Mexico's expanding population found jobs. Critics pointed out, however, that many of the plants did not observe the most elementary standards of health, safety, and environmental controls. Local authorities joined plant owners in preventing labor from organizing despite Mexican law. And the majority of workers were young women, often no older than sixteen.

The worst of the economic crisis barely seemed past when Mexico City was struck with a major earthquake. Hundreds were killed, thousands more left homeless. The government seemed incapable of response; for the first time, an outpouring of private initiative spontaneously took over, with individuals digging through the rubble to free the injured. For more than a year, hundreds survived in primitive tent cities on the medians of the city's wide boulevards. Even today, damaged buildings still stand throughout the downtown area.

Although the worst of the economic suffering was over by the end of the decade, the 1980s also witnessed the first real challenge to the legitimacy of fifty years of PRI rule. As in 1910, trouble began in the north, where the PAN, a conservative party committed to less government intervention in the economy, won several local and state elections. Too often, the PRI responded to apparent PAN victories with overt fraud and corrupt counts, despite earlier promises of free elections. As a result, PAN's popularity grew, less due to its position on the issues than because PAN became the symbol of integrity in the electoral process.

If 1968 demonstrated the end of the "Mexican Miracle," the elections of 1988 marked the end of political legitimacy in Mexico. For the first time, Mexican voters were offered a real choice of three viable candidates; for the first time, a candidate other than he who was hand-picked by the PRI actually seemed capable of winning the presidency. The PRI candidate was Carlos Salinas de Gortari, who had been named by the outgoing president Miguel de la Madrid. On the Right, representing the PAN, was Manuel Clothier, a wealthy industrialist. Clothier advocated a return to free enterprise, and tried to make honest elections his major issue. Far more threatening to the PRI, however, was the challenge from the Left, where Cuauhtémoc Cárdenas represented a coalition of smaller parties under the banner of the Democratic National Front.

Cuauhtémoc Cárdenas captured the imagination of Mexican voters as no candidate had for years. A former governor of the state of Michoacán and longtime PRI member, he had challenged the tradition whereby every Mexican president since the Revolution had chosen his successor. His father was the beloved Lázaro Cárdenas; his first name, Cuauhtémoc, commemorated the last Aztec emperor who died resisting the Spanish conquerors. The campaign was a populist one in the tradition of the Revolution, advocating a redistribution of wealth in Mexico's badly skewed economy, a hope for the thousands of slum dwellers, and a stronger government role in the economy.

Initial returns from Mexico City indicated a close election, with a Cárdenas victory likely. Then, the government announced the computers tallying the count had crashed. A week later, the government announced that Salinas de Gortari had narrowly won, with a majority barely over 50 percent. Cárdenas supporters immediately cried foul. In Mexico City there was talk of protest, even a possible coup. But nothing happened. Six months later, Salinas was inaugurated as president, but at a terrible price; for, no longer could the government even pretend that Mexico was an electoral democracy. Mexico was a one-party state, and elections were little more than a charade.

The Tumultuous Nineties

Throughout Latin America, the eighties became known as the "lost decade"; by 1990, most of that continent was worse off than it had been ten years earlier. Mexico was no exception. Meanwhile, on the other side of the world, Soviet Communism had collapsed, and there, too, capitalism and democracy were proclaimed the wave of the future.

Thus, Carlos Salinas became president of Mexico at a time when conventional wisdom almost everywhere argued in favor of new economic and political freedoms, free markets, and electoral democracy. In this new climate, Mexico, with its government-dominated economy, restrictive trade policies, and one-party state, was definitely out of step. What's more, the traditional policies were failing under their own weight. Mexico thirsted for new directions.

With substantial support from progressive elements in the PRI and from powerful business leaders in Mexico, Salinas decided to reverse the trends of forty years by moving toward a more open economy. Fortunately for Salinas, the United States had independently become fascinated with the notion of a vast free trade region that would encompass all of North America. Thus, both neighbors sought to break down the economic barriers that had traditionally separated the two countries.

Salinas was far more reluctant to take dramatic steps toward political democracy, perhaps fearing the opposition of more traditional elements within the PRI, perhaps convinced that economic reforms must precede political reforms, or perhaps simply committed to the tradition of a one-party state. Hence, Mexico would follow the path of Chile and China, both of whom had apparently succeeded in opening up their economies without opening up their political systems—at least in the short term. Most Mexicans, understandably, were willing to try anything.

To be sure, the idea of promoting economic reform while clinging to a closed political system was not a new idea in Mexico; the dictator Porfirio Díaz had pursued a similar policy one hundred years earlier. Indeed, the Salinas administration was so aware of the similarities that its Ministry of Education rewrote the history books used in the nation's public schools to place the Díaz years in a more favorable light. Although the new history books received little attention abroad, the change was a significant statement: cherished values that had been associated with the Revolution for almost a century were no longer sacrosanct.

NAFTA and the Economy

Salinas' economic reforms were finally realized fully on January 1, 1994, when NAFTA, the North Atlantic Free Trade Association, went into effect. Negotiations had gone on for years; the treaty had only barely passed the U.S. Congress after long acrimonious debate and extensive lobbying on both sides. NAFTA (or the TLC, as it was known in Mexico, the Spanish acronym for Free Trade Agreement) envisioned one huge economic market extending from the Arctic to Central America that would tear down the economic barriers that had once separated Canada, Mexico, and the United States. For the United States, NAFTA reflected a daring expansion of its long-standing goal to enhance free trade throughout the world.

For Mexico, the stakes were even higher, as NAFTA represented the end of an economic policy crafted over almost a century. Its impact would also be more dramatic, since the United States is a far more significant trading partner to Mexico than Mexico is to the United States. NAFTA also represented the culmination of the economic policy to which Carlos Salinas had dedicated his presidency; he had implemented many of its provisions before the treaty even went into effect.

During the Salinas years, the face of Mexico's economy had changed drastically. Import duties were reduced; for the first time since the 1930s, manufactured products made in the United States were readily available. Mexican products became more available, although not on the same scale, in the United States. A curious Mexican success export story was Corona beer, a mass market brand in Mexico that was marketed as a premium product in the United States. Even more important to Mexico was the fact that foreign capital was now welcome in Mexico. American banks opened Mexican branches. Assembly operations were no longer restricted to the *maquiladora* on the border; Ford Motor Co., for example, began assembling most Escorts sold in the United States in the northwestern city of Hermosillo. The most visible impact was in the many new American retailers, from Wal-Mart to McDonalds, found throughout Mexico. Even Taco Bell was part of the new American invasion. And at the United States-Mexican border, huge lines of trucks backed up on both sides.

The treaty, itself, envisioned the eventual free flow of goods and capital across the borders of the three signatories. At the same time, in both Mexico and the United States, some issues were too hot politically to be included in the NAFTA free market, at least for the time being. For Mexico, this was petroleum, that longtime

168

symbol of national independence. So, NAFTA excluded free trade and foreign investment in the petroleum industry. For the United States, the exception was people. Although products can cross the border freely, people cannot, and this includes the drivers of the trucks that carry the products.

Even aside from the exclusions, NAFTA and its vision were controversial in both countries. No one could predict the long-term effect. In the United States, opponents of NAFTA feared a large-scale flight of jobs across the border into Mexico; after all, Mexican workers received less pay in an entire day than American workers received in one hour. In Mexico, opponents feared American interests would buy up the entire Mexican economy, making Mexicans strangers in their own land. Some, focused on the same differential in wages, feared that all of Mexico would become one huge *maquiladora*, competing in the global economy on the basis of cheap labor and minimal safety, health, and environmental standards.

Fears on both sides of the border have proved valid, though highly exaggerated. Factory jobs have fled to Mexico—and, sadly, probably would have fled there or somewhere else anyway. In Mexico, foreign conglomerates have bought into the most productive Mexican enterprises, driving smaller, less efficient producers into bankruptcy. Of more importance is the nature of the jobs that have been gained and lost. The United States, for example, has lost factory jobs, but increased employment in financial services and technology as a result of increased imports to Mexico. Mexico has seen factory jobs in the export sector skyrocket even while it has suffered a decline in small businesses. Then, what of the future? Mexico has yet to demonstrate conclusively that it can compete effectively beyond the level of low wages and loose environmental standards. At the same time, jobs do continue to flow to Mexico (as opposed to Asia, where wages are even lower), as a result of proximity to the United States and a highly-motivated work force.

Domestic Economic Change

In addition to reversing dreams of total self-sufficiency, the Salinas administration also moved to privatize Mexico's traditionally state-dominated economy. The government sold to private investors its interests in a broad range of economic ventures, from manufacturing to utilities. The size of government diminished. It was widely believed, however, that friends of the Salinas family and well-placed members of the PRI, taking advantage of inside deals, were the principal beneficiaries of privatization. Ironically, the widespread corruption that accompanied privatization greatly diminished any potential salutary effects of a more open economy.

The most risky economic "reform" of the Salinas administration was the elimination of the *ejido* and its privileged position in Mexican law and mythology. Since the 1930s, the *ejido* had been protected in law; *ejido* land could not be sold. Peasants living on the *ejido* were subsidized by government, who bought their production at inflated prices. Salinas eliminated both the subsidy and the protection and, henceforth, *ejido* land could be bought and sold like any other land. Critics feared unscrupulous landowners would take advantage of uneducated peasants, unleashing a new wave of immigration to the cities. Others saw in the elimination of the *ejido* the very symbolism Salinas intended: Mexico was becoming a full-fledged member of the capitalist world and a full-fledged participant in the global economy. Its unique institutions, derived from its own past, were history.

As a counterpart to the abolition of the *ejido*, Salinas created the so-called Solidarity Program, in which the government financed grassroots efforts by peasants and workers to work for their own economic development. The Solidarity Program was PRI politics at its best: the government decided which local groups would receive aid, those in need received government aid, and faith in the PRI as a political party was restored.

Corruption and Drugs

Corruption has always been an integral part of the Mexican political system. Since colonial days, one paid to have the law look the other way, and one paid to receive from government what was already an entitlement. Corruption on a small scale meant paying off the police officer who stopped you for a traffic violation. Or, paying a bureaucratic to process your paperwork before the next century. Corruption on a grand scale meant paying to receive the official permissions necessary to do business, or kick-backs in order to receive government contracts. Many labor leaders had become rich by accepting bribes to postpone a strike.

Corruption was pervasive, and everyone knew it. Lower-level officials paid their superiors for opportunities to demand bribes—and were obligated to pay those same superiors a certain percentage of the expected take. At the top of the pyramid, huge fortunes were made. Most presidents retired as multi-millionaires. One Mexico City police chief retired with a fortune of some $50 million on an annual salary of less than $50,000.

Under the Salinas administration, corruption reached new heights of daring and outrage. Privatization of government-owned enterprises seemed less a policy than an opportunity to enrich one's friends and supporters. Government became intimately linked to the most powerful Mexican conglomerates; friends of the administration joined a consortium with the American giant ADM to virtually monopolize the distribution of tortilla flour in some markets. During the Salinas years, Mexico acquired twenty-three new millionaires, all of whom were somehow connected with the government and with privatization. In total, Mexico could boast of having more millionaires than all of Europe.

To make matters much worse, during the early 1990s Mexico fell victim to the corrupting influence of the world-wide illegal drug trade. Traditionally, Mexico had been a minor player, exporting to the United States modest quantities of marijuana. In the late 1980s, however, the Colombian cartels decided to move their major transport route from the Caribbean to Mexico. Suddenly, Mexico became the major intermediary source of the billions of dollars entering the United States every year. Mexican drug families arose to manage the trade, some acquiring the wealth and exhibiting the brutality of their Colombian counterparts. They dominated entire towns and regions, owned high-level police officials, and paid off politicians. Many Mexicans believed their influence reached to the highest levels of the Salinas administration. No one was safe, not even the Archbishop of Guadalajara, who was shot down in broad daylight as revenge for his opposition to the drug trade. According to some estimates, drugs were second only to petroleum as Mexico's most valuable export.

The Zapatista Revolt

On January 1, 1994, the same day NAFTA formally went into effect, several hundred Maya Indians started a revolution in the remote southern state of Chiapas. Within a few hours the rebels, faces hidden by ski masks and armed with weapons ranging from shovels to machine guns, seized control of some half dozen towns, including San Cristóbal de las Casas, a tourist and commercial center. The disciplined young men and women occupied town halls, burned records, released prisoners, and kidnapped a hated former governor—but, they treated local inhabitants and tourists with respect. They called themselves the Zapatista Army of National Liberation after the hero of land reform in the Mexican Revolution of 1910.

Although taken by surprise, the Mexican government hoped to quell the revolt quickly with a massive display of force. Within days, a force of more than 12,000 men forced the few hundred rebels to retreat into the inaccessible rain forests of southeastern Chiapas. The rebels, though no longer a viable threat to anyone, had survived.

To the dismay of the Salinas government, what had started as a minor military action quickly became a public relations victory for the rebels. Somehow, the small rebellion touched a nerve among millions who shared their frustrations and lives of total desperation. Most Mexicans believed their grievances were legitimate. Their spokesperson, the self-styled Subcomandante Marcos—a well-educated, literate white—quickly became the darling of the media. He sent to the world via the Internet lengthy protests against conditions in Chiapas, often accompanied with clever witticisms. His masked face appeared everywhere; in Mexico City, Marcos dolls were sold in front of the cathedral. Even Ed Bradley of *Sixty Minutes* slugged through the Chiapas jungle to interview Marcos. Marcos' immediate popularity was probably as much a commentary on the bankruptcy of the Mexican political system as it was affection for a man whose face no one had seen, a man known only by his nom de guerre.

Once barred from a military by the force of world-wide public opinion, the government agreed the rebels had real grievances and agreed to negotiate with them. Chief negotiator for the government was Manuel Camacho Solis. He was on the so-called Commission for Peace and Reconciliation and was one of the few members of the PRI upper echelon still widely respected for his integrity. Archbishop Samuel Ruiz of San Cristóbal de las Casas, respected by both sides, chaired the commission. Negotiations have continued off and on from January 1994 right up to fall 1998, when Archbishop Ruiz resigned from the commission to protest human rights violations by the military.

The Zapatista revolt remains important in Mexico not because the rebels ever had any real chance of winning, but because it brought to the national consciousness many unresolved issues of Mexico's past. Chiapas, itself, was a mystery in the minds of most Mexicans. It has played little part in the Revolution, and had not shared in the programs of land reform and economic development. Traditionally loyal to the PRI, Chiapas was ruled by an unholy alliance between PRI bosses and landowners; they did not hesitate to use force, whether that of the military and police or the irregular gangs of toughs financed by landowners, to keep peasants in line. Racial lines were more tightly drawn in Chiapas as well.

In other words, Chiapas represented the worst of traditional Mexico—land shortage, exploitation, racism, unresponsive government—confronting the worst of modernity. For, Chiapas was also rich in resources: oil, land, hardwoods and the repository of Mexico's largest rain forest. Consequently, the Maya peasants, already squeezed by the power structure, found themselves losing what little land remained to oil and government reserves.

Rebel demands were complex, and at times contradictory. They demanded that the government devote more resources to Chiapas, to which the government readily agreed; after all, spending money was the traditional PRI approach to discontent. But, the rebels also demanded political autonomy. This scared many Mexicans, even those otherwise sympathetic, for it implied a political breakdown of society along racial lines. Some critics compared the Maya demand for autonomy to the reservation system in the United States.

The Zapatista revolt concerned not only long-term issues for the nation as a whole, but also the very real question of the future of political power in Chiapas. Local landowners and bosses, determined to hold onto their power and land and determined to preserve the fear that had sustained their position for centuries, did not hesitate to resort to violence. Both local police and paramilitary forces under local bosses, sometimes in conjunction with federal troops, kidnapped, tortured, or worse those believed to be supporters of the Zapatistas. In December 1997, over forty men, women, and children were massacred by paramilitary forces, some of whom were identified as police. Ironically, those massacred were not Zapatistas but members of a religious group looking for peaceful solutions.

Perhaps the revolt's greatest accomplishment, however, was giving a voice to those who until now had none. It forced the government to take peasant and indigenous demands seriously. Among the rebels, themselves, women also achieved new respect. Not only did women serve as soldiers, commanders, and negotiators but, in rebel-held territory, new laws were implemented to end the traditionally male-dominated society.

From Salinas to Zedillo

The year 1994 was also one of presidential election in Mexico. During the previous December, President Carlos Salinas had named as his successor, Luis Donaldo Colosio, another economist. Colosio was an attractive candidate who campaigned on the issues of honesty in government and greater citizen participation in the political system. His chances were enhanced by the popularity of the Solidarity Program among the poor and by the initial euphoria of NAFTA among the middle class consumers, who suddenly found themselves with far more choices in the marketplace than ever before. The two opposition parties seemed unenthusiastic for another battle at the national level, and the PRI had built up an incredible war chest by adopting American-style fund-raising techniques. Once again, it seemed that the PRI's political acumen had come to its own rescue.

In May, however, Mexicans were shocked to learn that their next president, Colosio, had been assassinated while campaigning in Tijuana. The shock transcended the murder of a candidate, for Mexicans had assumed that their political system had become sufficiently mature beyond the realm of murder and assassination. Further assassinations occurred over the next nine months, including that of Francisco Ruiz Massieu, the PRI secretary general and former brother-in-law of Salinas, as well as several high-level individuals associated with the Colosio assassination investigation.

The gunman in the Colosio assassination was arrested almost immediately, but no one believed he was acting alone. Two theories abounded: according to the first, the so-called "dinosaur faction" of the PRI, those who were determined to hang on to the old ways, saw Colosio as a threat to the status quo and decided to get rid of him; the second theory attributed the assassination to drug lords. In one way or another, most conventional wisdom concluded that Colosio had fallen victim to the ugly underside of the Mexican establishment.

Two candidates were assumed to be likely replacements: Manuel Camacho Solis, the respected peace negotiator in Chiapas, and Ernesto Zedillo Ponce de León, a long-time PRI politician who most recently had served as Colosio's campaign manager. As it was Salinas who must decide, he chose the safe course and went with Zedillo.

After everything that had happened in recent months, the 1994 campaign itself was surprisingly lackluster. Between the Zapatista revolt in Chiapas and the recent assassination, most Mexicans seemed to have decided that they had experienced enough excitement for one year; better to go with the PRI, at least a known quantity. Ultimately, Zedillo won, garnering slightly over 50 percent of the vote.

However, the routine character of the 1994 election did not mean a return to the past; for, democracy was still an issue. Shortly after his inauguration, Zedillo witnessed the creation of the Federal Election Institute, a powerful independent body that would oversee the fairness of future elections. Unless the "dinosaurs" resorted to more violence, Zedillo was likely to be the last Mexican president to have won solely by virtue of being the PRI nominee. Moreover, television debates, introduced in Mexico for the first time in 1994, signaled that future candidates would have to be more telegenic than in the past; in this first round, both Zedillo and Cuauhtémoc Cárdenas, the candidate of the Left, appeared completely intimidated by the cameras.

By late December 1994, having survived an indigenous revolt and several political assassinations, the Mexicans grew weary.

But, the year was not over yet. In its last weeks, a severe run on the Mexican peso forced its devaluation to the point where once again Mexico faced virtual bankruptcy. Only a huge bailout from the United States and the International Monetary Fund saved the Mexican economy and banking system. The bailout came at an enormous price, however, for Mexico had to agree to a strict austerity program that severely cut into what social programs had survived Salinas' privatization; interest rates approached 100 percent. By 1998, it appeared that the bailout had worked (Mexico paid back the United States early), but most Mexicans would still feel the effects for years to come.

Unlike previous economic crises, the crisis of 1995 further threatened the credibility of the government and the PRI. During the intervening years, a consumer-minded middle class, encouraged by the cheap goods from abroad NAFTA had made available, had gotten itself deeply in debt by buying into a middle class lifestyle on credit. Now this lifestyle was threatened, as many found themselves no longer able to make the monthly credit payments under the new interest rates. Automobiles, electronics, even homes, were being repossessed; one bank in Guadalajara opened a parking lot where its debtors could drop off their cars and have their loans forgiven.

Thus, for the first time the middle class unified, forming El Barzón, a national debtors organization that held periodic demonstrations and refused to pay off loans with exorbitant interest rates. Middle class protest was both something new and something threatening. To make matters worse, many attributed Mexico's economic trauma not only to poor policies and bad luck, but also to corruption at the very top. During the Salinas administration, it appeared as if Salinas, his brother Raul, and his close associates had accumulated millions of dollars through corrupt deals and payoffs. For the first time, too, a former president was not only subject to criticism, but was forced to flee to exile in Ireland to avoid likely arrest. His brother, meanwhile, was arrested for corruption and ties with the assassinations.

As the Mexican twentieth century draws to a close, then, its government faces a crisis in confidence as severe as that which Porfirio Díaz had faced when the century began. Unemployment is high, violent street crime rampant, and malnutrition ever-increasing. Virtually everyone associated with the government is assumed to be corrupt. Informed Mexicans no longer look to government or the PRI for solutions, and buying favors can only go so far. Fortunately, this time Mexico has the option of revolution or a new dictatorship: electoral democracy in a multi-party state. Both the PAN and the PRD have matured into effective political parties, skilled in selecting candidates and winning elections. Both have been extraordinarily successful in state and local elections since 1994; even the PRI has come around to compete in elections, rather than to steal or manipulate them. The most striking single election occurred in the summer of 1997, when Cuauhtémoc Cárdenas was elected mayor of Mexico City, and the PAN and PDR together won over two-thirds of the seats in Congress. For the first time ever, Mexico is well on its way to becoming a multi-party democracy. At best, new leaders and new political structures will provide the time necessary to restore credibility, so that the government can begin to address Mexico's massive social problems in the twenty-first century.

AFTERWORD

As Mexico prepares to enter the twenty-first century, it confronts many of the same questions of a century ago. Can Mexico compete in free markets and within the global economy? Are Mexico and its leaders ready for multi-party democracy and free elections? Is Mexico capable of incorporating into mainstream society the millions who continue to live on the edge of existence? Will the United States treat Mexico as an equal partner?

It is easy for North Americans to read the story of Mexican history and come away feeling smug and self-satisfied. After all, opportunity, democracy, and prosperity for the majority are no longer issues in the United States. It is important to remember that Mexico faced obstacles the United States has never faced, and has succeeded where North Americans still struggle. Mexico has been as successful as any nation in achieving a multicultural society. And, Mexico continues to face the mixed blessing of sharing a border with the world's most powerful country: "So far from God, so near to the United States," Porfirio Díaz is reputed to have said. Not only did Mexico lose half of its territory to its more powerful neighbor, but it continues to be at the economic mercy of the United States, which it can challenge only at its own peril. Recent years have created new problems, as some members of Congress have sought to introduce fundamentally American domestic issues—drugs and immigration, for example—into the United States' formal relationship with Mexico.

Today, Mexico is only beginning to become visible to most North Americans, as both its economy and its culture are assuming an increasing presence in the United States. Mexican music,

Youth, the future.

Mexican food (Americans now consume more salsa than ketchup!), and Mexican literature are all becoming an integral part of American culture. Americans of Mexican descent number almost 20 million, approximately the population of Mexico City; Los Angeles has the second largest Spanish-speaking population in the world. The United States, which has profited in the past from the contributions of the diverse populations of Europe, is today enriched by the growing number of Mexicans in its midst. In addition, many contemporary observers argue, the United States-Mexican border is becoming a world of its own, neither Mexican nor North American but a unique synthesis of both.

Yet, differences remain. There is no other "frontier" in the world quite like that which exists between Mexico and the United States. Nowhere else is the contrast in culture, tradition, and economics so stark. Perhaps these two countries may never fully understand each other, even as both adopt many of the pleasures and insights of the other. But, in order to coexist peacefully, myths, generalizations, and biases must be transcended that not only prevent understanding but can easily lead to hatred and fear. For, in a climate of hatred and fear there can never be winners, only losers.

But, there is much reason for optimism. The Mexican people, throughout their history, have exhibited a resiliency, an adaptability, and an ability to survive that has transcended the political institutions that have not always served them well. Their zest for life, their loyalty to family and friends, and their openness to new opportunities offer the promise of a better Mexico in the next century. North Americans, in turn, have always proven themselves to be far more generous and understanding when dealing face-to-face with individuals than when dealing with abstractions. Thus, as Mexicans and North Americans come to know each other better as individuals, not just as political entities or as "problems," there is the very real hope of partnerships not only between the two countries but among the two peoples. Cooperation, after all, does not require sameness as much as it requires both peoples to view differences as opportunities yet undeveloped.

Other Illustrated History titles from Hippocrene. . .

Ireland: An Illustrated History
Henry Weisser

Erin go bragh! While it is easy to appreciate the natural beauty of Ireland, the Emerald Isle's history is also a rich and complex subject of study. Spanning prehistoric and Celtic Ireland to modern times, this concise, illustrated volume examines the people, religion, social changes, and politics that have evolved into the tradition of modern Ireland. Henry Weisser takes the reader on a journey through Ireland's past—to show how historic events have left an indelible mark on everything from architecture and economy, to the spirit and lifestyles of the Irish people.

Henry Weisser received his Ph.D. from Columbia University and is a Professor of History at Colorado State University. He has taught Irish history for many years, and has led groups of students and teachers on trips to Ireland. He is the author of seven books, including *Hippocrene Companion Guide to Ireland*, *Companion Guide to Britain*, and *USA Guide to the Rocky Mountain States*.

166 pages • 5 x 7 • 50 b/w illustrations/maps • $11.95hc • 0-7818-0693-3 • W • (782)

Russia: An Illustrated History
Joel Carmichael

Encompassing one-sixth of the earth's land surface—the equivalent of the whole North American continent—Russia is the largest country in the world. Renowned historian Joel Carmichael presents Russia's rich and expansive past—upheaval, reform, social change, growth—in an easily accessible and concentrated volume. From the Tatar's reign to modern-day Russia, the book spans seven centuries of cultural, social and political events. This is a book to be enjoyed by a diverse audience; from young scholars to those simply interested in Russian history, here is the perfect gift idea, a handy guide for travelers, and a wonderfully concise yet extensive, survey of Russian history.

252 pages • 5 x 7 • 50 b/w illustrations • $14.95hc • 0-7818-0689-5 • W • (781)